THE PURPLE PILL

GOD'S CALL FOR HIS BRIDE TO MAKE HERSELF READY

ROBERT E. STATHAM

Copyright

The Purple Pill
God's call for His bride to make herself ready.

Copyright © 2017 Robert E. Statham

All rights reserved under International Copyright Law. No part of this book, text or cover, may be reproduced without written permission from the publisher.

Published by GooseBear Press
www.GooseBear.com
@GooseBearPress on twitter
Editor: Marie Stille
Assistant Editor: Allesa Statham
Cover design, media, and content layout by GB Media

Unless noted all scripture taken from the Holy Bible, NEW INTERNATIONAL VERSION ®, NIV ® Copyright © 1973, 1978, 1984, 2011 by Biblica, Inc. ® Used by permission. All rights reserved worldwide.

To contact the author about speaking at your conference or church, please contact via twitter @RobertEStatham or visit www.robstatham.com

All GooseBear Press books are available at

Christian bookstores and distributors worldwide.

Ebook ISBN: 978-0-9996959-0-6
Paperback ISBN: 978-0-9996959-1-3
Library of Congress Control Number: 2017918457

Printed in the United States of America for distribution worldwide.

Table of Contents

Dedication............................... 7
Author's Note........................... 9

Chapter 1 Introduction................. 17
Chapter 2 The Mirror.................. 21
Chapter 3 The Enemy.................. 41
Chapter 4 The Call..................... 55
Chapter 5 Inside Out.................. 71
Chapter 6 The Invisible Wall.......... 91
Chapter 7 The Maze................... 103
Chapter 8 The Process................ 115
Chapter 9 Your Purpose............... 131
Chapter 10 His Order................. 147
Chapter 11 His Kingdom.............. 163

Author.................................... 175

Dedication

I thank God almighty for everything, for gracing me abundantly with words and the wherewithal to follow Him through this entire process. I dedicate this book for God's glory and ask His blessing settle on all whose eyes grace these pages.

I would also like to thank everyone that encouraged, helped, supported, and shared with me in writing this book. You know who you are. There are more people than I can name here. I will say the top on the list by far is my beautiful wife Lesa and our children Jedidiah, Faith, Hope, and Charity.

> He who finds a wife finds what is good and receives favor from the Lord.
> -Proverbs 18:22

Lesa, I love you and thank you so much for loving me and always telling me the truth. You are the best thing in my life by far. God has used you to make me a better person. You have taught me how to love, work, laugh, and live life. You are mightily used by God and I benefit from it more than anyone on earth. My children may be able to argue with me. Everywhere you go God's blessing and love flows. I look forward to our blessed, prosperous, and long life together.

Dedication

My children - Jedidiah, Faith, Hope, and Charity - you are gifts from the Lord. God has plans to use you mightily in this life. Only you can limit what He has for you. I love you with all of my heart. Thank you for sharing your love and childlike faith with me every day. It has changed me for the better. I admire each of you more than I can put in words. Jedidiah, never lose the passion God has given you and always use it for Him. Faith, my "go getter," the first to help. Nothing can stand in your way. Hope, my blessed dreamer. I love your imagination and gentleness. Charity, my performer. God will use your talent to share His love everywhere you go. I pray God's perfect, good, pleasing will unfolds in all of your lives as you grow up.

Without all of you I couldn't have penned this book, for God has used my family, friends, and acquaintances to teach me these truths I share. May God bless you and keep you always in the shadow of His wings.

Author's Note

This book is for anyone who wants more out of life. It is for those who feel the doldrums of life have hemmed them in. There is a God given hunger growing in your spirit that has not been satisfied. We live in the most exciting times the world has ever seen and God has great plans for His bride to show the world His goodness and His love. We must understand our part through His divine purpose created before the creation of the world, and then be led by the Spirit to fulfill it. This results in His glory and our greatest blessing. God is good, all the time!

First let me back up and share what qualifies me to write this book. I will cut to the chase - I do not have a doctorate from an ivy league school, or from a seminary, or a string of letters to follow my name. I have not spent 30 years as a pastor or full-time minister. In fact, from the world's perspective, I don't have much to impress you in regard to my qualifications. I would like to humbly present to you that is exactly who God qualifies. I am much like Gideon, just about the last guy in the world people would pick. God is in a habit of choosing people that are not qualified in people's eyes to do His work - Joseph, Gideon, David, Samson, Ruth, Esther, me, and you. God plus my clay vessel is all He needs. I knew

Author's Note

the credibility I'd gain if I had Shawn Bolz, Bill Johnson, Joel Osteen, Mark Hankins, and Andrew Wommack contribute in the foreword because I love those guys, but as much as I love them and feel like I know them unfortunately they have no idea who I am :) Therefore, I am certain that if you continue reading it will be by faith, believing God has something for you, not because you're impressed with my education or spiritual giants I rub shoulders with or have taken a selfie with. Thank you for having faith in God! I am confident you will find your heart touched by the revelation He unwraps as you're filled with a newness of life you have been thirsting for. I am a living testimony that He can use foolish and weak vessels to bring His amazing truths to light here on earth. **To Him be all glory.** You are in good hands – His!

I was born the youngest of three brothers in 1964. My Father was a career United States Marine and one of the biggest blessings in my life. My Mother was loving and kind. My parents, for the most part, were happy but lived at best a distant life from God. I could probably write another book about my childhood but I will save that for a later time. After a distinguished career my Dad retired from the Marine Corps and moved to his hometown of Cheyenne, Wyoming when I was a teenage boy.

I graduated from High School and attended the University of Wyoming. I spent the better part of 6 years, off and on, going to school for a

The Purple Pill

degree that would help me make money but I never knew what I was supposed to do and thus I never did it. On November 2, 1988, I confessed Jesus as Lord of my life and believed in my heart that God raised Him from the dead, and I was born again (Romans 10:9-10). My life seemed to go from black and white to color in one day. I knew my life had changed and I was hungry for more. More of God, not more of school.

I was swept away in the current of life and never completed my degree. Four or five, I can't remember, classes from a degree I decided to take a semester off to earn money. Well, a car payment later, and I never made it back. I went to work at a Christian Radio station. I loved it. I started working part time 2 hours a week and quickly moved up to News Director – full time days. The best you could do there. Then I had my first significant encounter with God after being saved. He told me to leave the radio station. I didn't want to, but I did.

I couldn't find a job. The car payment was now coupled with a house payment and all the expenses that go with it. No job. No money. About 2 months after leaving the radio station at God's direction. My small savings was gone and I was in my living room, in tears, praying. It went something like this, "God I thought you asked me to leave my job? Forgive me if I was wrong (tears streaming). My house payment is due tomorrow and I don't have any money?!?!? Forgive me, PLEASE HELP!!" As

Author's Note

I rubbed my eyes sniffling my phone rang. It was a friend of my older brother. He owned a construction company. He asked me if my Dad still had a truck with a snowplow. Yes. He asked if I would like to move snow that night. Yes. I borrowed my Dad's truck, moved snow all night. Wore out, without sleep, at 8 o'clock in the morning I was handed a check that paid me more than I made in a month at the radio station. My house payment was covered and I slept peacefully knowing there is a God in heaven Who loves me!

For the next 10 years I worked construction. I worked my way up from part time labor to full time equipment operator. Within time I was given the opportunity to become a partner. We sold the company in the late 1990's shortly after I went to work for a large oil company doing pipeline inspection work. Again, I moved up to an office job taking care of regulatory compliance. This is where I first started a life of looking at evidence and understanding why things fail.

In 2004 I married my beautiful, lovely bride who is the biggest blessing in my life. Over the course of the next ten years we were blessed with four beautiful children.

In 2006, expecting our first child, I decided to start my own company helping people perform regulatory compliance and failure investigations. God blessed me with a great partner in that company. It took off. We went from busy to really busy. I traveled training and performing investigations everywhere. It was exhilarating. God changed my life. He showed me how to look into the mirror of truth. Doing that sets you free.

Things were going great. We'd been in business for 10 years and decided to attend the first Charis Business Summit. I thought it would be a good time to get away with the family and be exposed to new learning opportunities. I was attracted to the Leadership speaker, Dr. Dean Radtke. I was not disappointed. If you struggle with effectively delegating then you need to go sit under Dr. Radtke's teaching! Drop the book and go! He is anointed. There were other breakout sessions, one for real estate and the other marketing. I had no real interest in either. We did have a couple rentals so I opted for Billy Epperhart's Real Estate session. The first thing I heard was "you cannot serve both God and Money" (Mt 6:24). I immediately sat up. TRUTH. I love how truth gets your attention. He went on to share how God has put us on this planet for a purpose. He talked about making sense of making money for making a difference. God was revealing His purpose for my life. I had never really wanted to be rich. I just wanted to be comfortable and take care of my family.

Gazing into the mirror of truth I saw how selfish I had been. God wanted to expand my vision. He doesn't just speak to you, God speaks through you. I saw how He had positioned me to fulfill my purpose and that I

Author's Note

really didn't know what His purpose for me was. He began to show me why I was created. I lit on fire and burned with joy, excitement, and freedom! You will too when you figure out why God created you for this time in this place.

To make a long story short my wife and I created a company to help redeem communities by making "Investments that Make a Difference." We use various vehicles to invest in one thing – people. We use real estate to help people transform from renters into owners. Along the way we build relationships and share through coaching, training, and mentoring. It is useless to talk about the Kingdom of God if people never experience it. We are able to introduce people to His Kingdom up close. He opens the eyes of peoples' hearts and they begin for the first time to see His purpose for them is much bigger than they had ever imagined. Our job is to bring His Kingdom by imparting the blessing He has given us to everyone we do business with. Our work is profitable beyond a profit and loss statement leaving a legacy for the future.

I believe the bible is the inspired, infallible, inerrant, living word of God. His word is living and active and has changed my life forever for the better. It is more than I can recount in a hundred books. For years I ran around the religious mulberry bush looking to bring people to church instead of bringing Jesus out of me to people. I had the truth but I didn't rightly divide it. I was dull of hearing. I said the right things but I saw no power. I was living in a rut. His Kingdom is all about righteousness, peace, joy, and power (Romans 14:17 and 1 Corinthians 4:20). There are no ruts in His Kingdom. I know my experiences shared in this book will help you understand the subtle changes needed so you can hear and know His purpose for your life, which brings freedom, life and life in abundance!

Heavenly Father I pray for everyone reading this. Thank you for every reader. Spirit of God give them wisdom and revelation. Enlighten the eyes of their hearts to see and understand. Give them spiritual ears to hear and the wisdom to tune out the noisy distractions that would keep them from your presence. Lord we worship you, we love you, as you reveal yourself to all reading this may they be filled to overflowing with your joy, which is our strength. May Your Kingdom come and your good, perfect, and pleasing will be done in our lives, in our families, in our friends, in our churches, in our communities, just as it is in Heaven. Thank you, Father, for calling us to be a part of your body, your bride. I know you have great things planned for each one of us and I ask you to reveal that purpose and plan. Lead us to glorify you and walk in your blessing. Use us to bring your Kingdom everywhere we go.

I ask this all in the mighty name of Jesus. Amen and Amen!

God Bless you in Abundance,

Rob

Author's Note

One

Introduction

WORDS,
Create pictures in your mind,
Imprints upon your heart,
And ultimately determine your destiny.

My purpose penning this manuscript is to share words with you that help create God's picture of your life that will imprint on your heart and create a beautiful destiny. The results will be seen by the world around you - who will see the glory and goodness of God. The words in this book are a result of my walk with the Holy Spirit to share the experiences, insights, and truths He has revealed. Fulfilling my destiny to help you accelerate as you advance in fulfilling yours. Living in His Kingdom showing yourself to be His disciple. I love Jesus. Everywhere I turn, in the Bible, at work, at home, and in my heart, I see Him repeatedly providing a way out of the mess we find ourselves in. God's grace and purpose for this book is to empower strengths and cover weakness. Far too often I find myself in a mess that I'd really rather not show anyone. A mess I'd rather not even admit I'm in. A mess I wish and pray Jesus would just save me from. Too often we find ourselves cornered in a tomb with no way out in desperate need for Jesus to show up, call our name in a loud voice and say, "Come out!" Then, like Lazarus, we find new life and step out of our mess and leave the grave clothes behind.

We are living on the precipice of the greatest revival the world has ever seen and it is coming through people, like you, hearing the Spirit of the Lord calling them into their divine destiny. Before divine destiny comes divine alignment. Life comes as we position ourselves to receive and fulfill God's purpose for our individual lives.

God's sets you free, matures you, anoints you, and then leads you to give and impart what He's given you to the people around you.

My prayer for you is that God's Spirit will impart to you the loving plans He has to prosper you, give you a hope, and good future as you walk with Him free from the distractions of the enemy. May God break every chain the enemy's tried to entangle you with. That you take your place, and play your part as God ushers in the greatest revival ever. May His Kingdom come, His will be done, right where you are and everywhere He sends you on earth, just as it is in Heaven! Freedom, Love, Joy, and Peace await you in abundance. Read with ears to hear His Spirit. May He grant you the Spirit of Wisdom and revelation as He opens the eyes of your heart. May you realize the incomparably great power He has for you, that you may be a king on this earth ushering in His Kingdom for His glory, and your blessing.

    In Jesus name, Amen!

Two

The Mirror

"NO man has a chance to enjoy permanent success until he begins to look in a mirror for the real cause of all his mistakes."
- Napoleon Hill.

    In the 1990s I worked industrial construction as an equipment operator, backhoes, cranes, dump trucks. A group of us were on lunch break in a tool shop at a plant and a guy said, "Did you hear about the guy selling brains?" "No," we replied. He begins telling us there was a salesman at the plant office selling brains. We looked at each other with a grin of expectation as he continued. The salesman had an appointment with the leadership of the plant and gave his "brain" presentation. It boiled down to brains being offered at different prices. He said, "I have laborer brains for $2 a pound,

The Mirror

pipefitter brains for $5 a pound, and engineer brains for $20 a pound." The President of the company asked is that all he had? He replied, "Well..., I do have corporate executive brains, but... they're $2000 a pound!" The shock was evident, $2000???!! Smugly he inquired, "Why so much??" The salesman replied, "Do you have any idea how many corporate executives you have to kill to get a pound of brains?" We all roared with laughter. I have often told that joke and adjust it to the audience. The humor is always well received. I share that with you now, not talking about construction workers but Americans in general. It is odd the higher up the ladder we go it seems the more we have to place our brain in stasis.

I just got off the phone with our local light, fuel, and power company. We had a renter move out October 31 and we showed up the next day and to our surprise the power was off. My wife called them to understand why the power was off as we have a landlord agreement with them. This means if a renter moves out they won't turn off the utilities they will just begin to charge us. They explained that our agreement does not go into effect unless it is winter which begins (in their minds) November 1. The renter moved out the day before and they run over and shut off power, hmmm? Makes sense to anyone who has had their brain placed "on hold" for most of their life, right? Remember, I said, "I just got off the phone with the power company." Well, that is because after three online attempts and two phone calls over the course of five days in an effort to turn power back on, they finally decided that my wife doesn't have that authority. As I sat there on the phone talking to a very nice man named Greg. He was very polite. He had a pleasant charm and mastery of our language and he took 15 minutes to do what a six-year-old knew should have been done a week earlier. In fact, the six-year-old would not have shut the power off in the first place.

The reason I share the humor with the power company experience is because we ALL are in desperate need of assessing ourselves in light of common sense, in light of common grace, in light of truth. In fact, the only way things can improve is to see the need to change for the better.

Eyes are useless when the mind is blind.

The problem that feels like a millstone on the individual's neck is they do not see how they can help, it's the company, the system, or rules they can't change that have bound them. If you interviewed the power company employee, Greg, I know he would tell you how none of what happened made sense. But then, he would also tell you how they were following the rules, systems, processes, and flow charts that they were hired to follow. Greg would be describing a dilemma that we all know too well. It makes an individual feel powerless to effect the right change. This affects all of society but for my purpose I am concerned and will focus only on the body of Christ and you, the ones who worship in spirit and truth.

The Mirror

There is a supernatural stirring that is going on. There is a spiritual call being sounded in the heavenlies and those who have ears to hear have a growing hunger for something more than what they've experienced. Their heart knows there is something more, something better. God is stirring believers deep within their hearts, and calling them into alignment. The hunger inside is fruit of the stirring in their spirits to rise to His call. To hear His Spirit and fulfill God's purpose then we, and the world around us, will see the bride of Christ transform and be found without spot or wrinkle, so the world will see that there is a God who loves them and pours out His grace and redemption on anyone willing to receive it. **This will be the greatest revival in the history of the world.** God is bringing His Kingdom of light right here on earth as it is in heaven. He is doing it through His people. He is stirring you now to fulfill His divine call on your life for you, your family, your city, and your nation.

In this book, you will hear the call being sounded that only your heart can hear. It is time to heed your call and have clarity on your purpose. You will also see the opposition facing those standing with God Almighty's banner over them. For that banner represents His Kingdom, His rule, His dominion. The dilemma is what I shared above - you may see the problems but how can one person make a difference? I will share with you the steps needed to deal with that dilemma and be a light in a dark place. The result will be you walking in a new-found power of purpose, love, and grace which will also result in Jesus using you to aid in the church, His bride, to make herself ready. The first step is to look in the mirror to see an accurate reflection by gazing into the mirror of truth. The mirror is His Word. Individually and corporately we will be transformed into a bride without spot or wrinkle, ready to meet the Bridegroom.

Wisdom equips us to reign in life. We cannot afford any thoughts that are not His. Opinions don't work, yours or others - we need His opinions. Guilt, Shame, Regret, and Bitterness cripple. Our bodies respond to us - mentally, emotionally, and physically. Most people have trained themselves to hide the part that is unforgiving and bitter. While a few may walk around spewing bitterness like acid out of the mouth some science fiction creature in a Godzilla movie. All these attributes do is cement a bond inside to the past which drains life. Break the bonds of the past. The Bible (Romans 8 and 1 Corinthians 3) tells us we own things present and things yet to come, but NOT the past. The past has been bought by Jesus. Your past is not yours, it is His. Our shift in identity starts here. Think what God thinks. Be free. You are not governed by opinions of people. You are governed by the opinions of God. You are content which means current circumstances will not rob your joy. The joy of the Lord is your strength. You were designed to reign in life.

Since 2001 I have taught and performed failure investigations mainly in corporate America. These are catastrophic events like flares overfilling causing a fire, injuries, and sometimes even loss of life. Horrific tragedies. If anyone could have connected the dots and seen the accident coming then it certainly would have been avoided. The issue is people can't see the forest for the trees. Hindsight is 20/20. Investigating after something has happened by gathering all forms of evidence and recreating the event is an incredible experience - in fact it is life changing. People begin to see an accurate reflection of themselves and their company in the mirror of truth. That is what evidence is - it is truth manifested in our lives. In this case it is a fire, flow rates, decisions to open valves or close them and when. It goes on and on, but evidence always leads us to understand what happened. I love doing that because I help people learn from things that go wrong. In order to learn from things that go wrong I HELP THEM CHANGE THE WAY THEY THINK. The process implemented by a company results in helping individual people understand and experience a change within their very heart. All companies, all churches, all cities are made up of individuals - people. These people live together forming the entity and somehow lose the understanding how to effect change outside of themselves for the good.

It's not readily apparent to everyone that the reason things go wrong is because they played a part in it. The critical word here is "part." It may be a very, very, very small part, but it is still a part. Most people tend to think it's bad luck, or worse yet it is someone else's fault – blame. Until we SEE the small part and change it, only then will we see the bigger part change. Let me share an example closer to home. We have friends that always seem to be fighting to make ends meet. They are on the verge of being impoverished and think they just need more money, but in reality, they need to change the way they think. The big part they see is being impoverished. The part they play seems invisible to their eyes. They are impoverished because of wrong thinking, wrong sowing, and wrong believing. They are struggling due to the choices they have made in the past that have led to where they are now. One example would be buying a giant t.v., instead of setting aside some money for an emergency. The problem is they didn't connect the dots that their one decision, and a whole bunch just like it, is the cause of their lack.

But in order to minister to what they need we must first give someone starving a sandwich BEFORE you have the opportunity to minister to what they truly need. We will only temporarily help them if we don't give them what they need - a different mindset.

How does this apply to you, our church, and our country? Here's the bombshell; We need to change. Mark Twain once said, "The only person who likes change is a wet baby." Today, I encourage you to be open to new things - God has new things in store for you. When we are not willing to change, we wear a rut in life holding on to what God did in the past instead of changing and moving forward into what God is doing now. We cannot continue to do what we have been doing and hope for different results. Philippians 1:6 says, "He who began a good work in you will carry it on to completion until the day of Christ Jesus." That is a wonderful verse. I hear people use that verse often to encourage people that are waiting for God to move. God is waiting on us to move. He is cheering for us to get in the game. To get in the game we must change the way we think. God told me this and then showed me the "why, what, and how" that needed to change.

> Romans 12:2 instructs you "to be transformed by the renewing of your mind."

Rob's translation says you need to change the way you think!

Our friends think they need more money but like many lottery winners you see - more money just postpones being broke. It doesn't change anything. It's like a band aid, not a cure. In fact, they end up worse off. God wants the best for you. The end of Romans 12:2 says,

> "God's will is good, pleasing and perfect."

In order for God to give you your heart's desire you have to change the way you think. In other words, **if you continue to think the way you have been thinking, then you are hindering Him from giving you what you desire**. Wrong thinking is actually described as a stronghold in the bible (2 Corinthians 10:4-5). That is what we are to tear down using the weapons He has given us.

The Purple Pill

In Matthew 16 Jesus said the he will build the church, and the gates of Hades will not overcome it. That is good news. I have shared a little humor to highlight a battle we are part of. The enemy is raging at every level of society to get people in a place where they feel helpless to effect positive change.

Okay, back to step one - an accurate assessment or looking in the mirror. We must see where we are at in order to learn not to repeat the same past failures. This book is written with a forward-looking perspective, through God's eyes, laying out your good future. Before we discuss what is coming there are a few things we need to "see" in order to look into the future. The world we live in and the world we see are not the same thing. The world we see is a reflection of a world we do not see, a spirit world. The two together make up the world we live in. This world is often blind to the spirit of darkness wreaking havoc. The church is immersed in lethargy and suffers from not seeing much better into the spiritual realm than the blind world they live in. This is changing. The enemy must be exposed and light flood where darkness tries to hide.

Imagine for a moment you have the power of invisibility. Think of the things you could do, the places you could go, and no one could stop you. You could fly free forever. You could tell people things that could help them or terrify them. The thoughts are endless. The power and influence is almost unthinkable. Well, the devil is invisible and he is strangling the body of Christ with our own belt. Using a twisted belt of truth, he misuses scripture in an attempt to bring confusion and doubt. Ultimately trying to have us credit God with evil that is the devil's. His goal is to disconnect the body from the head because the body of Christ is the only threat on this planet stopping his free run to steal, kill, and destroy (John 10:10).

The first thing we must do is to look at the big picture, then look to see how we play a part in that picture.

The Facts

"You can spend your whole life building a wall of facts between you and anything real."
— Chuck Palahniuk

The American Time Use Survey shows the average adult spends 20 minutes a day doing civic/religious activities. The majority of time, outside of sleeping and work, is spent watching television/entertainment at 3+ hours a day. We find ourselves strapped for time and bombarded with more choices to spend our time on than any generation in history. This war over our use of time is clearly seen in the church. Attendance of believers is slowly dwindling as more and more born-again Christians believe they are better spending their time somewhere other than in church. A current assessment of the Christian church in America reveals a whole bunch of small bands of believers living in silos they call church. The evidence of the enemy's attacks is seen by our silo and the belief that isolation is protecting us and the gospel of truth, when in reality isolation is robbing us. Our strength is in relationship with the body, not isolation. Our blessing flows when we walk in unity, not isolation (Psalms 133). The lie that has infiltrated the church model, isolated and alone, that our small (in the big picture) band of believers are doing church right and have God's complete message. This is what renders us powerless and the world sees it and knows it. The adversary throws fuel on the fire encouraging us to celebrate when we lure people from another silo to ours. We somehow take solace that we're growing. It is growth, but this methodology more closely resembles cannibalism than evangelism. The enemy laughs as we devour ourselves and think we're better off. Resulting in more disunity and building thicker walls in our silo.

The letters from Paul in the new testament, always refer to the church at a city. Not to the individual silos within the city. He certainly mentioned church in small groups and churches in homes, but he always addressed the church that is the gatekeeper of the city. The church at Ephesus, the church at Antioch, the church at Rome, and so forth. The results we see in the Bible is a church walking in the love and power of Christ. The church we see in our cities can more accurately be described as one without power. The thought that unity is going to come by all the other silo's watching as your individual church transforms the city is plainly wrong. It is evidenced by a lack of fruit. The obvious fruit of those beliefs is disunity and

The Mirror

pride. Pride that our church is better than the one down the street. Those thoughts are not coming from God's heart. I say this because they are not in the Bible. That is a problem.

That is an assessment from the outside. Let's look inside our church. Let's look at our value system. Our value system is what is reflected in our church. We read Acts 2:38-41 where the believers devoted themselves to the Apostle's teaching, fellowship, the breaking of bread, and prayer. Their numbers grew daily! Then we continue down a path of isolation. Most, not all for there is always a remnant, have pursued church as being Sunday morning. This consists of coming together with little or no time to truly fellowship and share what is happening in our lives - good and bad. Isolation. The deception of isolation is that it brings protection. This is seen in Genesis 3 with Adam and Eve. They hid from God. They isolated themselves. The lie of darkness is that staying away from God's light, or hiding, helps us. I'm not trying to suggest churches are trying to hide from God. They are trying to hide from evil through isolation. This does not bring protection. These actions aid the enemy because our only hope is being exposed to the light of God and exposing the world. We are a city on a hill and meant to shine. Remember before the fall how Adam and Eve were naked and felt no shame. They didn't want to hide. The world tells us to "never let them see you sweat." God tells us to come to Him as we are and He will give us rest.

Communion has gone from a sit-down meal in

the name of the Lord (see 1 Corinthians) to a sixty-second ceremony begging God to forgive us and help us do better - it has turned into a ceremony of works. I pray to God that we don't realize the next step of an evil plan to turn communion into a purple pill that will fix everything. **Relationship is the purpose of communion.** We must sit down and break bread together in remembrance of Him, then instead of hiding we share our heart with others. The push to shorten this time cultivates isolation not relationship. The wrong thinking is if you don't see my shortcomings then I'm ok. That is a lie. I'm not ok. I need a Savior. I need to be forgiven and cleansed white as snow. I need to boldly approach the throne of grace, not hide from it. When we expose our shortcomings to God and the people around us, then we are living a real life and being set free as we walk in the grace Jesus provided. We have been driven by attacks of darkness to hide from relationship which is also critical to effective discipleship. In fact, it is impossible to make disciples without intimate relationship.

The enemy then tries to replace the mandate of go make disciples with a push for an increase in numbers. Invite people into church is the mantra. We invite people to church to make ourselves happy. This doesn't accurately line up with the command of Jesus to "Go and make disciples." We now say, "come and be a disciple." Discipleship is on the verge of being a lost art. Relationship and covenant have been forsaken for invitation and faithfulness to our silo. This way a person can put on a smile and go to church

The Mirror

Sunday seeing people yet remaining isolated. That doesn't sound like God, does it? Growth only comes in being discipled - relationship. Showing your heart and trusting it won't get stomped on. All other models result in stagnation. Why is there such a push for numbers? Is it motivated by the Love of God within us wanting the best for the people around us? I hope so, but wonder....

I can plainly see that motivation seems to get replaced by jumping to the end result of just needing to grow - numbers. Numbers help in tithes and offerings, but not much. Barna statistics show the "numbers" in church aren't very generous. Around 20% regularly give or tithe 3 or 4%, not even close to a tithe of 10%. All Bible believers know a tithe is 10%. Jesus talked about the wise man hears the word and puts it into practice. Others listen and get swept away by storms of life. We often get sidetracked in discussions that tithe is not in the new testament and it is in the law which we've been set free from. Of course, the tithe was before the law, it was Abraham. The same Abraham Galatians says that we are his children by faith and we have the same blessing that was on Abraham. We know God loves a cheerful giver, unfortunately most are not cheerful but give out of a sense of obligation. The fruit of giving out of obligation is emptiness. You'd be better off to not give. God doesn't need your money. He loves you and wants your heart because only then will you be set free and happy. He knows you cannot serve two masters or you will die. Money is a quick and easy way to see where our heart is.

God loves a CHEERFUL giver because they understand God is their provider and money is nothing but a tool he gives us to provide and bless. The push is to worship the provision and not the Provider which is evidenced by the statistics.

This pressure to grow is fueled, unfortunately, by a basic need for the church to provide for the pastor instead of a hunger for intimate relationship and a love for each other. Providing for our pastor is certainly biblical, but again truth and motives are under attack and being twisted by the enemy. **What brings tears to God is these dedicated, faithful men called to shepherd and guard the flock being attacked from every angle with little to no help from us - fellow believers.** There is a spiritual call, a sound going out that is calling us into alignment to honor those serving us - this is our opportunity to bless God.

In order to combat evil, we must see it, let me point out some of the volleys being poured out on God's church and His gatekeepers, our pastor's. We know God's gifts and call are irrevocable, yet 80% of pastors are out of the ministry within 5 years. A few may have been misguided to dive in to the call, but I know a vast majority have heard the call of God and are being faithful to His voice. Unfortunately, pastors are devoured much like kids eat chicken nuggets. In the place of honor people influenced by darkness sow dishonor. The world has little to no respect for pastor's because they watch how God's children treat them. The enemy finds weaknesses and exposes sin to fire the rage, and the whole time we then place an expectation on pastors of perfection. Those expectations are impossible to live up to. A majority of people judge others by lofty expectations and themselves by their intentions. Dishonor then is reflected in our giving. We don't look at giving as what it is, but that we are giving in exchange for a pastor to perform - tickle our ears, give us goosebumps, quail dissatisfaction and acts of the flesh. That is not a gift. When you give and expect to get something in return then you are buying not giving. A gift is given without expecting anything in return. If you give with expectation of someone owing you, then you are going to be disappointed for your reward has been crushed. You are not giving according to a cheerful heart, to those in need, to those God leads you to. You are giving like the world does - giving to get. Shame on us. We watch as a spirit of poverty strangles our pastor's. We try to help by pushing for numbers. The numbers then are asked to sit and watch, not grow and be transformed. We are caught in a vicious cycle that is void of our only hope - God and His love.

    We are waiting on God to move all the while we have benched and quenched Him by our actions and beliefs. If we don't see a move of God then we label our pastor's and church's as "missing it." Thinking we need to hear something fresh and this pastor is the "same old stuff." **God cannot move in our lives if we do not act in faith on His word.** Sitting and waiting in a pew is not even close to stepping out of the boat. We then go in search of a new church/pastor that says what we want to hear, and the cycle starts all over again - cannibalism. God help us.

Our pastor's feel an overwhelming pressure to perform and meet needs that cannot be met and the frosting on top is poverty and desperation for finances. Every parent on earth has a desperation inside them to take care of their family. Pastor's must meet that God given desire first or their dignity is torn from them. The enemy aims at the fabric of our hearts and we (people) sometimes help him. My wife and I are ready to jump on the devil when he kicks the front door down and shows up with a pitch fork, horns, and pointed tail. The fundamental problem is the enemy shows up using me, or her. This requires discernment and a heart open to repent and follow God and His love in everything. This requires a loving relationship. Pastors are ready to whip the devil too, but when he shows up as poverty due to believer's not believing the scriptures that clearly tell us to be givers. This derails a pastor more often than all the other attacks combined. The Barna Group said:

> "The average person, when feeling pinched for time or money, will focus too much on the thing they're missing and too little on the future. Their strategy for getting back on their feet and living past the crisis is faulty or missing. They borrow from the future, both by literally borrowing money on unfavorable terms and by thinking they can delay the

undelayable (for example, spending time with their children)."

We live in the world and take a couple hours Sunday to honor God, thinking a bath (washed with the water of the word) once a week is working. Waiting and saying we're ready to get serious when we see God really move. Until then, we'll give a little and wait. Confused why over 80% of Millennials want nothing to do with today's Church? Why kids are lost, hurt, and dying? Why God doesn't do something? He has done EVERYTHING. He has sat down and is waiting for His enemies to be made a footstool. We wait on God while He waits on us to believe Him and act like it.

We value ourselves and others by how much money we make. **God says you are priceless, therefore you are priceless.** Do not ever think your value is based on your bank account. If you value yourself that way then you value others that way also. This is not right and is keeping you from your heart's desire of intimacy and life with God. Do not ever think your value is what the world sees - the world is blind. Open your eyes. See what God sees. You are priceless. When you believe that, you will act like it. You will see the value He sees in people, and people will see God in you. He will be glorified and you will be blessed. You are priceless - receive all that He has for you and bring His Kingdom where you live, work, and have your being. It is time to tend the garden God has placed you in.

The Purple Pill

My brothers and sisters, this is ALL EVIDENCE of the work of our enemy!

I know I just pointed out all the things we like to ignore. Hoping these problems will go away or solve themselves. Or worse yet, that it's not our fault - we didn't play a part in it. Other people need to change. That's a convenient lie as you sit there a victim of others' actions with no control. I think we may sit next to each other in church (tongue in cheek). This is a very poor strategy that plays into our adversary's hands. It does not work. God calls you the victor!

> Now is the time for believers to assess their nation, city, church, and themselves through the lens of God's word, God's grace, and God's Love.

1. We must accurately assess gaps between what we are and what we should be based on these truths.

2. Then we must act according to that truth in love.

Deception comes thinking that merely listening to the truth helps, it doesn't. Doing it helps. James says this perfectly:

> "Do not merely listen to the word, and so deceive yourselves. Do what it says."
> -James 1:22

Think of the Israelites in the days of Moses.

There was the land of Egypt, or how it was. The promised land, or how it should be. And the desert between the two - the land of transition. This is a fabulous land to cross through, but a terrible land to settle in. God's heart is to renew your life to move into the promised land.

Prayer

"Father in heaven, please open our eyes that we may see what you see, hear what you hear, and do what you're doing. I pray we are not ones who settle in transition but we are led by your Spirit as overcomers into our divine destiny. As I read the rest of this book prayerfully highlight what I need to hear. Lord give me the grace to get out of the rut of the past and glorify you living life in abundance.

In Jesus mighty name, Amen!"

Three

The Enemy

"OUR greatest fear should not be failing, but rather succeeding at things that don't really matter..."
- Francis Chan

    I think we can all relate to the struggle we face dividing our time and not letting our schedule dictate our lives. I am convinced the easiest and simplest tactic of darkness is to simply distract us with being busy so we do not invest in what brings us life and glorifies our Father in heaven. There are thousands of great ideas, but we hunger for God ideas. If the enemy keep us scheduled to the hilt then we will pursue some good ideas but miss what brings us, and the world around us, life.

The Enemy

One stark truth the bible reveals (2 Corinthians 4:4) is that Satan has blinded the minds of unbelievers. The term unbeliever naturally leads you to think about the lost. The lost are certainly unbelievers. I also see many Christians that are unbelievers to some extent. In 1 Peter 5:8 we learn that Satan prowls around like a roaring lion seeking whom he may devour. The enemy is trying to imitate the Lion of Judah and when we believe that God is against us, or trying to devour us, then we have a real problem of unbelief. For over and over the goodness of God is revealed in scripture. Romans 12:2 tells us God's will is good, perfect, and pleasing. There is no devouring people in that, yet people still wrongly hold beliefs about God that are false and end up leaving them in bondage and fear. Unbelief will kill you. Remember the man in Mark 9 who told Jesus, "I do believe, but help my unbelief?"

Help us Lord with any unbelief in our hearts. What is your part or "how?" is a natural question that should come to mind. What is our part and how do we respond in a right way? In Matthew 16 Jesus warned the disciples to guard themselves against the yeast of the Pharisees. The yeast of the Pharisees is their teaching. It is lifeless and worse it renders, like yeast, the whole batch lifeless. I define the term "religion" as taking the Spirit out of God's truth and leaving only a lifeless shell. Outward appearance looks fine but produces no life, no love, no fruit. There is an air of pride at how good we are. There is a void of freedom, and of love, which is a void of God's presence. Religion are acts void of

The Purple Pill

God trying to reach out to God. Confused and lifeless people either decide to leave and go about their life or grind it out in the name of faithfulness. You have seen them, or maybe you're one of them, they do the same thing for twenty or thirty years and scowl at anyone who suggests a change because they are faithful! It is really very, very, sad.

Religion takes a hold of God's truth and twists it just enough that it actually brings death. The Pharisees had the very same ancient manuscripts that Jesus had. Jesus stands to read from the Prophet Isaiah (Luke 4) and they are amazed at the power and authority they witness in Jesus. He didn't read anything they hadn't heard before. He read it without mixing it with the same yeast that affects the whole batch of dough. I think of it this way. It is like sitting down to a Thanksgiving dinner and putting Novocain on the mashed potatoes. In no time, you can't taste anything. This is a dangerous place to be, for an enemy can dish up a spoonful of dung. Numb and unable to taste the difference people just eat up.

The charge to us is to guard against the twisted teaching of religion. The enemy wants to deceive well-meaning saints into mixing just a little yeast, religion, or Novocain in to the teaching of God's word.

> We have to be able to tell the truth to each other or we might as well quit, there won't be any sense trying to tell the world we're

speaking the truth when they can clearly see we won't tell ourselves the truth.

The question that should be burning in your heart and mind right now is "If religion uses the same scripture Jesus did then what is the difference? How can I not fall into the same trap?" That is a question with a very simple answer. Jesus was motivated by LOVE. God is Love (1 John 4:8).

The moment the enemy entices us to act for any other reason than love then we have fertile soil for a spirit of religion to grow. The outside appearance becomes the focus, wrongly thinking this has any effect on our heart. Religion then is off and running. The enemy advances taking territory on both sides. He promotes the church to isolate themselves to avoid the pain caused by people's hearts being torn in church splits. This results in a spiritual silo and pushes the lost further from a hypocritical church with a banner raised that says, "love your neighbor," but a lifestyle that says come to the silo of our isolation from society then we will share our conditional love. Jesus was not about isolating himself from society or from the synagogue. In fact, he embraced both and they were changed by His Love.

Let me share an example. A common message shared out of Ephesians 4 is the five-fold ministry. It was He who gave some to be apostles, prophets, evangelists, pastors, and teachers to prepare God's people for works of service. This is vital and true for His body to grow to maturity, yet when we are in a mindset to perform works of service and we're not motivated by love then we are strengthening a religious spirit which is lifeless. The glamour wears off rather quickly. We grow weary. Look for another church, or worse yet we hunker down and keep grinding. We keep telling ourselves that we're the faithful ones. The whole time thinking, if not speaking, that the ones who left are wrong and missing out. We grind, and grind, and grind never really tasting life or joy or peace. We scowl because we're faithful! The spirit of religion presses others into service. The vicious cycle wears a rut that is familiar and void of life, void of His newness and excitement of love.

The enemy fuels the fire of disunity. Contrary to scripture and using the weapons of the world Christians speak badly of other Christians/churches rather than speaking to them in love (see Ecclesiastes 10:20 Proverbs 18:21, and Matthew 12:36). This furthers disunity and strengthens the silos that promote isolation the church sees as protection. Now the enemy can sprinkle pride in our thoughts and words that our church is better than the one down the street. Deceiving ourselves. The leading thought process in the religious community is our church (silo) has the real message and all these other silos down the street will waste away and finally give in to our greatness.

Evangelism has been replaced with the gift of

cannibalism. Devouring ourselves and thinking we are better off. We think watching other churches get ripped apart through quarreling, sin, and disgrace somehow helps us because we absorb those same people??? God's word clearly says that when one part suffers we all suffer (1 Corinthians 12:26). This is like looking down and seeing our big toe has gangrene and the rest of the body celebrating that it's the toe and not them. If the toe suffers then the whole body is suffering. May God please open our eyes!

We have turned communion into a sixty second ceremony begging God to forgive us and help us do better - it has turned into a ceremony of works. I am sure the enemy will try to introduce a purple pill that is communion on the go. **Our microwave society is trying to produce a microwave Christianity to fit their itching ears and busy lifestyles.** No need to even pause with a cracker and thimble of juice, just pop this Jesus pill and you'll make it to heaven one day. The whole time the enemy runs rampant devouring our youth, stealing, killing, and destroying God's property entrusted to us - the earth. Please remember when Jesus took the bread and the cup and said, "Do this in remembrance of me." The "this" He was referring to was not a purple pill, it was not an oyster cracker and thimble of juice. The "this" was the Passover. The Passover feast, celebration, has been replaced in our rituals with a momentary pause to ask God to forgive us AGAIN? The Passover was first celebrated coming out of Egypt by the Israelites and passed down for generations. The lamb who takes away the sins of the whole world was Jesus. Jesus became the greatest act of love in the history of the world. He said, "Do this" meaning sit down and revel, remember, celebrate, my love for you that sets you free and makes you a child of God, for Jesus became sin for us that we might become the righteousness of God! Friends, it is time to sit down and commune. It is time to remember what He has done, to relationally worship Him. A time to grow together as His body. Not a time to stare at the back of someone's head. It is certainly a time for God to speak to us, but please remember we are not alone, we are not a silo, we are a part of a body - a body made up of people. People God loves. A relational God who uses people on this earth to minister His will, His love, to make His enemies a footstool!

Once religion has numbed us, then rather than tapping into the spring of living water (John 4), we try to look better than the world, concluding we just need to invite people to come into our silo to find what we've found. It is not living water. The power of testimony, as the woman at the well demonstrated, is sharing life with others that helps them find freedom. When love is not the motive but obligation because the big silo is the anointed silo we nullify the life love brings. Often, we invite people to church to make ourselves happy. It does not work. It leads to frustration. We pray that God would have people flock to our silo on a Sunday morning like moths to a flame. That would be awesome except most people are smarter than moths and a flame casts more light than a dusty silo. A silo is a modern

The Enemy

day bushel and we weren't called to hide our light under a bushel. People flocked to Jesus because He was God in the flesh, which means He was love in the flesh. People flocked to love, not a form of religion. This is the key to everything God is doing in these last days.

> "The love of most will grow cold."
> -Jesus

The enemy turns people away from love and drives them into acting like ravenous wolves. Congregations devour pastors like kids devour ice cream cones. Thinking we need to hear something fresh we then expect and even demand our pastor bring better and better revelation. The expectation is wrong because God brings revelation when we need it. If we do not act on the last word from God, why should He send a new one? James 1:22 tells us not to merely listen to the word and deceive ourselves, but to do what it says. **We convince ourselves, contrary to scripture, that it is what we hear that will change us**. That is a lie from the pit the enemy uses to bind us and destroy God's shepherds. We either move on (leave the church) and take as many "enlightened" ones with us, because if more people see the same thing then we feel better, or we move the pastor on. The same pastor we thanked God for sending to our church two years earlier. The same pastor we hugged and told him how much we loved him and anything we could do to help, that's what we're there for. That pastor. How do you think he feels? Please stop for sixty seconds and think about how that pastor feels and what he has experienced? What are his prayers? What were his dreams and what are they now? How do you think his children feel? How many times do you think his wife would like to repeat that vicious cycle? Please don't speak life and life in abundance out one side of your mouth and be an instrument that is ripping the heart out of His bride the next. We must love each other before we can love the world. We must love our pastor and let God, who is love, live through us as we choose life and blessings.

We celebrate numbers of people instead of the transformed lives of disciples. There is a mindset that numbers reveal God's anointing on a church. This comes about from the throngs of numbers that followed Jesus. Numbers are not the sign, the motive attracting the numbers is the sign of God's anointing. The motives for the crowds following Jesus was to press in to His love, to be set free from bondage, infirmity, poverty, and sin. The motives for many people flocking to the happening church is because others are flocking to that place. The numbers tell you nothing. The heart reveals everything. I think of God sending Samuel to the house of Jesse so he could anoint the next King of Israel. Samuel saw Eliab, Jesse's eldest son, and thought this must be the one. Then God told him people judge by outward appearance, "but I judge by the heart" (1 Samuel 16:7). It is not a sin to celebrate growth, but please see what God sees - their hearts. It is always a matter of the heart.

The Enemy

The adversary always plays both sides. He deceives us to act from motives other than love. We taste the lack of life and despise it. The enemy then tells us our answer to what our heart yearns for cannot be found here, and then promptly directs us to press into the world and what our flesh yearns for. We still do not find water to quench the thirst in our heart but find temporary amusement from our pain. The devil's happy, we're miserable and he tells us it is the church's fault, our parents fault, the democrats, the republicans, the Muslims. He tells us the fault lies outside of us, and therefore we cannot change it. We have no way to fix it. We are helpless and destitute. We slide off into a world that has no real meaning. We take a couple hours Sunday to honor God, hoping a bath (washed with the water of the word) once a week is working. The entire time our hearts cry for the love that never fails.

Are you still confused why generations that are coming up want nothing to do with today's Church? Why kids are lost, confused, and dying? Why God doesn't do something? Our children are very perceptive and see that we say "love" but we do not live by love. They see hypocrites and they are not afraid to share their opinions. God loves them and He longs for them to enter into His Kingdom because He loves them. God's motive is love because God is love! They desperately desire to experience God and this love that never fails. There are 65,000,000 Millennials longing to drink the same water Jesus offered the woman at the well. They are still looking for that spring of living water. That spring resides in you if you are born again and sealed with the Holy Spirit, BUT it will never flow out of you without love. You get wet first, then you can share it. It flows by love, not by want.

> "Work harder" is great for a sluggard but it is a lie for all others. Most people need to think differently.

I must also mention the enemy's push to destroy us from within. We live in a country opening our arms to Muslims who believe peace only comes by killing enemies of Allah - that is you and most of your friends. This is not the same peace Jesus brings. This is the same word but evil is what hides behind it. The devil came to steal, kill, and destroy, but Jesus came that you may have life and life in abundance. In his book Gaining Heaven's Perspective Julian C. Adams said, "The spirit of religion is the ugly thing that blocks the ears, eyes and sense of touch of the church and renders her ineffective and powerless." He then shared warning signs of a religious spirit:

- Inability to take correction and rebuke. Being defensive and argumentative, acting hurt and the refusal to submit to authority.
- Our prayer life becomes mechanical. We feel relief at the end of our prayer. We pray the same thing at the same time every day with no spontaneity.
- Defining the Christian life in terms of performance rather than the heart. (Discipline and will power are good, but when we take pride in what we do the religious spirit will

take root in our lives).
- We begin to feel closer to God than others.
- We feel our group is on the cutting edge.
- We have a critical and judgmental spirit.
- Leadership becomes bossy, authoritative and intolerant.
- We are given to exaggeration about spiritual matters.
- We try and make physical manifestations occur in every meeting, every time. (In fact, this drives away the presence of God and the power of the Spirit is nullified).
- If you are thinking about how someone else should hear this teaching rather than you, then it's likely that you have a religious spirit!
- If God's word does not pierce your heart and affect you, it is a sign that you have a religious spirit at work in you.

My friends, this is ALL evidence of the work of our enemy! This is all evidence of our lack of living by the Spirit. His Spirit is the Spirit of love for He is love!

The ultimate problem is the way we in the church define ourselves. We can listen to the world and the god of this world, the devil, or we can listen to Almighty God, the Living Word, and His holy scriptures. He is love and His church is the ecclesia—His called-out ones, His government on the earth. Called out to love and bring life to a hurting, dying world. Not called out to be another religious institution that does good works but rings hollow lacking in love.

The Purple Pill

In the book of Kings, Jezebel was a queen in the days of Elijah the prophet. She led her husband King Ahab away from worshiping Yahweh and establishing idol worship instead. Jezebel led the entire nation away from God into selfishness in search of God. She had cold-bloodedly killed many of God's prophets, His voice for the people. Today we can recognize the same spirit of Jezebel is at work in our nation. Boldly opposing the remnant of believers that still hold to worshiping in Spirit and in truth while also anesthetizing others to sit back and even join in idol worship of self. Evidenced by greed, division, and even hate. The forces of evil are attempting to immerse the church in a lethargy where the status quo is to listen to the word, but not do what it says. Comparing ourselves among ourselves is not wise and plays into the hands of our invisible enemy. Beaten down, our confidence is low and a Christian without confidence is like a race car with no fuel. We have to wake up and see ourselves as part of the problem. We have to bring His Kingdom to combat the gates of hell and spirit of Jezebel trying to destroy our children and generations to come. I urge you, I appeal to you - stand up for the Truth! **Stand up, in love and humility, for Jesus.** No longer will we quench the Spirit, no longer will we grieve the Spirit. We will no longer merely listen to the word, but we will do what it says! We walk in the footsteps of Jesus - we walk in love. We don't just read the greatest commandment, we actually love the Lord with all of our heart, mind, soul, and strength. We love our families. We love our neighbors. We

The Enemy

love at work, church, the grocery store and anywhere else the Spirit of God leads us. We live our lives today for Him, we look forward to the day we are face to face with our Lord and Savior Jesus. He gently, lovingly gazes into the depths of our being and says, **"Well done! You have been a good and faithful servant. Come your reward awaits you."**

To mark this as a day things begin to change in your favor let's put these truths in action. Please think of several people and/or circumstances that you can speak blessings over according to love. Read 1 Corinthians 13 if you need some help to get your mind moving. I will give you one - your pastor. If you have to get on the phone or Facebook to reach out then do it. Do not think of a list and wait to exercise His heart through your words and actions. This is simple; when you think of someone then act. If you need help coming up with names then put yourself on the list. It is critical you know what you're sharing with others is for you too. Love your neighbor as yourself. Complete this and your heart will feel like it's glowing with warmth. It is food for your soul when you do what He says. Well done!

Four

The Call

ALIGNMENT

> "Those who cling to worthless idols forfeit the grace that could be theirs."
> -Jonah 2:8

I love the story of Jonah for a myriad of reasons. It is a memorable story to start with, but what I am drawn to is the greatest revival the world, at that time, had ever experienced. Over 120,000 people turned to God and avoided judgment. The most amazing thing about the whole story though is that Jonah did not once tell the people to repent. Not one time. For three days, he walked through Nineveh proclaiming, "Forty more days and Nineveh will be overthrown." Essentially, he said it is over! See ya! But the people heard him. They believed the word of the Lord. They aligned themselves with God by turning from their ways and turning to God. God then revoked His sentence and showed them mercy. They did not cling to worthless idols and in turn found God's grace. Those that cling forfeit God's grace.

No one can walk in the things of God - love, joy, peace, prosperity, health, etc. - until we destroy the image of self, lack, poverty, and sickness. The wrong image is only replaced through the truth of the living Word. We see a reflection of our self in everyone we know. People are often negative towards others because they're negative towards themselves. Most cannot even see what they are doing. We project our value on others by bubbling out in all our forms of communication - over 70% does not even use words. This can be the posture you take around someone, or ignoring them, etc. The whole time it is actually a dose of what we think of ourselves. There is nothing wrong with this unless what you see is not what God sees - the truth. If you see what the world, devil, or in-laws see - a lie, then you are in trouble. Out of order, out of balance, and clinging to worthless idols. **Any beliefs you place over and before what God says is an idol and steals His grace from your life.** We must align ourselves with God and quit forfeiting His powerful Grace.

Alignment consists of Position and Purpose

Different segments of the church will cry for revival at different times. They are expecting God to move and release revival like the days of old. They expect God to move. The reality, and history proves this out, revival comes when people change - not God. God is the same yesterday, today, and forever. He doesn't need to change and He isn't going to change.

Let's look at Jonah's stomping grounds and what took place at Nineveh. The message wasn't to repent. The message was you have 40 days and Nineveh will be no more, but when the king heard this he gave a decree to fast, turn from their evil ways, and pray. Jonah 3:10 says:

> "When God saw what they did and how they turned from their evil ways, he relented and did not bring on them the destruction he had threatened."

Do you see it? They changed. They aligned themselves with God. It goes on to say that Nineveh's population was 120,000. That is quite a revival!

Throughout history you will see people, by God's grace, discover a revelation into His word that was there before. All that changed was people finally saw it, then they aligned themselves with God's truth. It happened in the 1700s with the the Great Awakening in the American colonies where George Whitefield drew incredible crowds preaching salvation freely offered in the Gospel, saying at the end of his sermons: "Come poor, lost, undone sinner, come just as you are to Christ."

Revival only comes through alignment with

The Call

God. All revivals start with people aligning themselves with God's truth. Not one started with some outpouring of the Spirit like raindrops falling out of the sky that you have no control over. God meets you where you're at and then calls you to follow Him - Align yourself with what He is doing. Remember the children of Israel were told that they had to dispossess their enemies before they could possess the land (Numbers 33:53). We, like them, have some work to do.

At a Wealthbuilder's event early January 2016, I had the privilege of hearing Dr. Lance Wallnau speak. Lance is funny, anointed, and prophetic. He shared a word God gave him that Donald Trump was God's anointed - he had placed a Cyrus anointing (see Isaiah 45) on Donald Trump. God would use a man for His purpose even though the man does not know God. I glanced at my wife and said, "Wow! Well, we can hide in the bushes and watch." You see at that time Donald Trump was an absolute joke. No one thought he had any shot of ever winning the nomination, much less the office of President of the United States! The strangest thing happened in that moment, even stranger than Lance uttering that Trump was God's anointed, was, for some odd reason I believed it. Now I look back and see it was the Spirit bearing witness. I was like a Ninevite hearing the word of Lord from Jonah - I believed it and it changed me. That was the beginning of God aligning me with His will.

In chapter 37 of Ezekiel the prophet

describes a vast valley full of dry bones. Ezekiel prophesied to the bones and as he spoke the bones began to move. They began to **align themselves** bone to bone and then he saw tendons, flesh and skin cover them. Dead bones aligned themselves and flesh grew over them but there still was no life in them. God told him to prophesy to the breath and he did. Breath then entered them and they came to life! They stood up on their feet - a vast army.

    This is a great picture of the church today. All of the things we described in chapter one are dry bones. God calls us to align ourselves with Him. I cry out, like Ezekiel did, "Dry bones hear the word of the Lord: Align yourselves in the body. God will make breath enter you and you will come to life!"

    Psalms 133 tells us how good it is when God's people are in unity, for that is where the Lord bestows His blessing. There are blessings from God that we can only receive when we are where God has called us to be. Unity does not come from all of the leg bones living in the south end of the valley. Unity comes when the leg bones align themselves with the hip bones, and so on. It's only through alignment that the body of Christ, the bride, can stand up in all her glory, spotless and without blemish. The alignment God is calling us to will release His blessing like we have never experienced before. We are living on the precipice of the greatest revival the world has ever seen and it is coming about by people hearing the Spirit of the Lord calling them into the correct alignment. Before life comes we

The Call

must position ourselves to receive it or it will pass us right by and we won't even see it.

Purpose

"The two most important days of your life are the day you were born and the day you find out why."
-Mark Twain

I believe Mark Twain was a prophet. No one recognized it because he wasn't a prophet in the church, God had him shaping American Literature. I know his take on purpose is profound. I remember finding out my purpose and it felt like a new lease on life. Almost like I was born again again, if you know what I mean. It was an awesome day! Unfortunately, I am in the minority of experiencing that, while most are just trying to be better than everyone around them - which is a trap. You will never be better, you will never be worse. You are different. That is why God doesn't talk to two people the same way. God has designed us uniquely different yet similar with His purpose knit in the fabric of our heart.

Albert Einstein once said, "Everybody is a genius, but if you judge a fish by its ability to climb a tree, it will live its whole life believing it is stupid." I talk to quite a few believers from coast to coast and border to border and a common theme I see is 4 out of 5 struggles with who they are - their self-perception. The world and the enemy have pushed tons of fish into believing they should climb trees and the reason they are no good at it, the reason they hate it, the reason they are lost in a sea of many who try to climb the tree but can't is because they aren't good enough. They don't have what it takes. The enemy comes with his native language of lies to steal and one of his top targets is your purpose. Andrew Wommack said, "If you want to destroy a man's vision, give him two." This is what each one of us are up against. Fish trying to climb trees are out of alignment, wrong position and purpose, and they do not even know why they were created. They don't know their purpose. They are in a dry and weary land with no water - but there is lots of company. The enemy encourages us to scream for God to do something! God has done something. I want to clearly speak into your spiritual ears, "Align yourself with God! Ask your heavenly Father what He created you for, what is your purpose?" This is the path that leads to life and life in abundance. One obvious answer you'll hear and find in scripture is He created you to walk by faith. Without faith you cannot please God. You cannot be aligned with God and struggle in a life influenced by the world, the devil, and anyone else who wants to hang their agenda on you.

Walking by faith is critical but it is also a high-altitude answer. God has specifics for you. To know if our dry bone is in the right place we better ask the Creator. Look at the intricate detail God went to just designing the human eye. The human eye can differentiate between about 10 million colors and is capable of detecting a single photon (the smallest measurement for light we have.) You see His attention to detail in

The Call

all of creation. The way a human body works together is awesome. Do you think He put any less thought into you? Into your gifts and your call? Your God given gifts and call reveal your purpose. Romans 11:29 says that God's gifts and call are irrevocable. That means He doesn't change His mind. He knows what you were made for and it is good; good for you, good for those around you, good for your community, and good for your nation. God even said, "It is very good." The only problem we have is most people don't have a clue what they were made for. I am including born again Christians. You have unique gifts for your calling, this day in history, the results are your greatest blessing and His greatest glory!

Very few people are fortunate enough to actually discover and fulfill the purpose God created them for. Those who do know are the ones who experience life at a level others rarely hear about, much less see. The fortunate ones start to take notice of the passions within them, and see the alignment of their skills and abilities. They see what they hate is actually what they have an answer for, and an anointing to bring here on this earth to help people. These fortunate ones also quickly recognize that what's in them and what they are designed for lines up but does not overlay. Another way to say it is they have some work to do. They must grow into their destiny. They then pursue their destiny with all their heart. God smiles as they find His plans of hope and prosperity.

Most are in desperate need of a boost along

the way. Some need to start at step one to understand that God has a plan and a purpose. Others are hung up somewhere along the way. The good news is He has a plan for me and I am right in the middle of fulfilling it. I help people like you find and fulfill their destiny. You have been led by Him to the right place. I pray you have ears to hear what His Spirit is speaking and it finds good soil within your heart that you might reap a hundredfold harvest.

You can do anything, but you cannot do everything. Choose to do what God already planned for you, then you will discover your purpose.

My desire to write this down is so that you can also share in my discoveries, my joy, in finding your purpose in life. When you understand your purpose then your life will change. You will go from living in a rut day to day hoping something will change for the better to living a life full of joy unspeakable, freedom, and passion. God will be seen on the earth through you! He will receive glory through fulfilling what He has called you to. It is much like a flower blooming in Spring. It is beautiful and everyone knows and thanks God for His wonderful creation.

> "The earth is the LORD's, and everything in it, the world, and all who live in it."
> - Psalms 24:1

GOD DOES NOT NEED ANYTHING. He

The Call

created everything for you. If you don't know this please stop and go read the dominion mandate God gave Adam and Eve in the garden (Genesis 1:27-31). He gives you everything you need according to His riches in glory.

Often people think knowing your purpose then doing it is easy, that is until they try it. All sorts of obstacles, hurdles, and walls seem to appear along the path. If these obstacles are not viewed through the right lens and conquered, then these obstacles act as a detour and may become a destination or a place one can settle without ever fulfilling their purpose. Unfortunately, 80% of people settle and never fulfill their purpose.

Fear not, you are not a settler, on the contrary, you are called to be a pioneer. You are going past settlers and are the 20% that discover and walk in their purpose. God's Spirit is going to give you a boost and help you over any obstacles to understand the purpose God has for you in this time and place. You're not a settler. This is your map to help guide you as you fulfill your purpose and walk in the life and life in abundance God has for you. The things standing in the way of you fulfilling your purpose can be overcome and must be overcome. Your spirit will testify that it will not happen by your power or might, but by His Spirit. God does not play favorites, but God has put a process in place to help you reach and fulfill your purpose.

To get in alignment with God you must first take notice of what He has knit into the fabric of your being for that is where your purpose lies. How? That is a great question so let's reflect on these statements:

- God knew you before the creation of the world. He knew you when He knit you together in your Mother's womb. He knew your time in history, your family, and your gifts and talents.
- Your life journey formed your values and perspective which led to gift discovery and development: **This is what you do best and what you love to do most.**
- Maturing is the process of how experiences like jobs, finances, marriage, family, and life forms you.
- Your PURPOSE is revealed when your gifts, talents, and acquired skills converge with a role that empowers you to do what you do best and love to do.

This intersection of your calling and your actions in line with your purpose yields Abundant Life! If you look that up it means ridiculously more life than those around you!!

Four bullet points makes it sound so simple - it is and it isn't. If we could remove the enemy and the obstacles of our fallen world you would see it is so simple you would need help to get it wrong. This is the point where I must discuss what we set our eyes on.

A word of CAUTION: As you focus on where God wants you and what He has for you to do - alignment and purpose - be certain to focus on Him. Your calling is what feeds you. This is all about the Father, Son, and Holy Spirit - His

Kingdom, His Will, His Way. The enemy will try to get us to focus on ourselves rather than on our God, our provider, our healer, our all in all. The enemy will try to counterfeit the things of God but they will be void of supernatural life. God is inviting you to come and serve Him by fulfilling your purpose which will result in bringing His Kingdom and His will right where you live, work, and have your being on earth. Our focus is always on God - NEVER FORGET THAT.

What We set our Eyes On

> "When you take your eyes off your nakedness and failure, insight provides identity, and foresight provides destiny, which are the two keys to living a prophetic lifestyle."
> - Kim Clement

I desperately wanted to replace "a prophetic lifestyle" with "an abundant life!" in Kim's quote, because some people get so tripped up when they hear the word prophetic, but I left it. I know in Kim Clement's eyes, and mine, they mean the same thing. A prophetic lifestyle is a life of faith which is abundant life. Kim, a prophetic instrument of God, was the first to introduce me to how people, human beings, actually "see." **We see with our body, soul, and spirit.** We are not limited to only our natural sight. With natural eyes, we see the world all around us. Examples would be what we see in our driveway, our mailbox, our bank account, or in the bathroom mirror, etc. The second way we see is with our soul through insight or our mind's eyes. Examples would be taking two or more things and putting them together yielding understanding. Your bills in the mailbox plus the balance in your bank account yield insight that you have more than enough. This can be applied with scripture, people's actions, the list is endless. For instance, seeing through people's facade at church. In short, you are able to see below the surface. You're seeing truth that is covered or not readily visible. The third way we "see" is the best way - we see with our spirit. This is described as the eyes of faith or foresight. **We see what God sees.** It is incredibly easy when what we see with our eyes confirms what we see with our mind and confirms what we see in our spirit - this usually only happens in hindsight. This happens after you have passed through the red sea. This happens after Abraham unties Isaac and sacrifices the ram Jehovah Jireh provided. Trust me, before the ram was revealed and they are walking up the mountain to worship when Isaac, Abraham's promised son, asks, "Father where is the lamb for the sacrifice?" Abraham doesn't see the ram with his natural eyes, and he may not even see the ram in his mind, but he assuredly saw that God would provide in his spirit. Hebrews 11:19 says "Abraham reasoned God could raise the dead." Abraham's sight contradicted God's word, but his insight was siding with God, and his spirit saw and believed God.

George Mueller said, "The beginning of anxiety is the end of faith, and the beginning of true faith is the end of anxiety." Believers have to believe. A host of believers want to **say** they believe but that is not enough. Faith is not a matter of talking, it is all about acting. Faith is seen by action, not words. You must believe and act on what God Almighty has told you over what you see, what your friends say, over what you might even think! God's word is true and until you stand up and act on what you believe, not on what you see, you will never walk in God's abundant life of faith. You will be bound by trying to mix the world's wisdom and ways with God's word. If you ask God to help you walk by faith and fulfill your purpose on this earth then He will. Just be aware you may, like I have, get backed into a corner and be tested to act according to what He says and you believe versus what is seen with natural eyes, what the world around you says, or what anxiety wants.

The working out of your calling can, and probably will, be in contradictory circumstances. The bible calls this faith. Look at Abraham, the father of many nations. Father of many nations??? He can't even have a child with his wife - contradictory circumstances. This is the battle of faith. It is critical that it is noted the battle of faith is grabbing a word from God and holding on in spite of what the natural eye sees. Some people are shipwrecked because they grab onto a good idea and just assume God will bless it. Grab onto His word and you KNOW he will bless it.

CALL TO ACT - ALIGN YOURSELF

Law of diminishing Intent - the longer you wait

to act on inspiration, the more likely you will not act.

Today may you be encouraged to evaluate how you use your time. Refocus your life. Let go of any distractions. Shake off the lies of the enemy. Shake off what you see with your natural eyes. Shake off any self-pity, discouragement, disappointments of the past and run your race with purpose. Redeem the time so that you can fulfill the destiny He has called you to. Prayer does not change things; prayer changes you and you change things. If you want to align yourself and fulfill your God ordained purpose, then you have to live by faith, not by sight. You have to fall into your loving Heavenly Father's arms and trust Him with all of your heart and lean not on your own understanding. The greatest commandment is to love the Lord your God with all your HEART, SOUL, and STRENGTH. Obviously, your heart can love. Your soul (mind) can love. Your flesh can love. It all flows from the inside out.

Prayer

"Heavenly Father have your way in my life. I love you. I trust you. I want everything you have for me. Align me for your glory. Reveal and confirm your purpose knit in my heart. Enable me by your grace to walk in it. Your will is good, perfect, and pleasing. Your glory is always my blessing. Help me walk by faith when the enemy comes, when my own eyes don't see

The Call

what my spirit knows.   May Your Kingdom come and Your will be done right here on earth as it is in heaven. Help me see what you see. Use me to move by love and set others free from bondage - physical, mental, or spiritual - for your glory and it's always my blessing.
    In Jesus mighty name I pray, AMEN!"

Five

Inside Out

"WORDS may show a man's wit, but actions his meaning."
- Benjamin Franklin

While sitting in an adult Sunday School class in a small rural church in 2008, I listened to twelve adults, and I use that term with teeth clinched, argue over "who's my neighbor?" We read the parable of the good Samaritan in Luke 10 and proceeded to get caught up in who deserved help and who doesn't. I sat there in stone silence. Each minute that passed made me feel sick. Why was I sitting there? They are arguing over who is their neighbor? Who they should help and who they shouldn't? They were justifying the way they live and using God to hide behind. I couldn't stand it. I was livid. I can't remember one word the pastor shared that day. My wife and I went home. I sat down in our living room, livid still, I opened my Bible to Luke, chapter 10. Saying out loud, "Who's my neighbor? Who's my neighbor!!?? WHAT A BUNCH OF MORONS!!!" Right as I finished saying "morons" I looked out our window. I pointed to my neighbor across the street and said, "That's my neighbor!!" He was standing on a four-foot step ladder trying to paint the eave of his house. Honestly, It looked dangerous. As I pointed and declared who my neighbor was I realized instantly that I have a ladder that would really help him, maybe I should even help him, I have lived there for over 7 years and had never introduced myself to my neighbor. My heart was crushed. I knew the Bible. I believed the Bible. I was a hypocrite! I wasn't loving my neighbor like myself. I hadn't even said hi. God showed me the gap between what I said I believe and what I really believe. Laid bare by the Holy Spirit, I stood up and walked across the street and introduced myself and offered help. That was the beginning of God peeling my heart and showing me the gap between what I said and what I did.

> That day I learned that behavior is the servant of beliefs.

Our minds can actually be blind to ourselves. Someone once said we judge others by their actions and ourselves by our intentions. There is much truth to that. We change the scale and don't even notice for we judge with such bias. I was livid at those "morons" that didn't know who their neighbor was, yet I was guilty of not loving my neighbor. I didn't see it until **I saw it in them** and applied it to myself. Every one of us has made a list of assumptions that we believe to be true. We have not tested each assumption. There is nothing wrong with this – as long as the assumptions we've made are correct. If the assumptions we make are not correct then we have a problem. Our foundation needs some maintenance and repairs. Have no fear for God is in the foundation business. He can help. He will help if you ask Him to. The sneaky thing about these wrong assumptions is they hide themselves in our barrel of truth. We don't think our assumptions are wrong until we see they are not based on the truth.

Truth demands alignment - truth demands change. Everywhere there is a gap is an opportunity to be more like Jesus and change by being led by His Spirit.

> The pessimist complains.
> The optimist expects change.
> The leader adjusts.

Let me share a story that takes place along the coast at low tide. An older gentleman enjoying the sea air walking along the beach notices a younger man walking towards him. Every few steps he bends over, picks up a star fish, and throws it back into the ocean. The old man thinks it's odd behavior and as they approach each other he greets him and asks him what he's doing, throwing star fish back? The young man replies, "They get caught in the mud at low tide and will die either due to the mud, lack of water, or hungry birds, so I toss them back into deeper water." The old man grins and says, "Young man there are thousands of star fish along this coast. You can't possibly think you can make a difference?" The young man reached down and picked up a star fish and tossed it into deeper water then said, "I just helped that one."

Where do we begin? Popular belief is you develop a strategy to reach millions then an effective movement will begin. That belief bypasses the timeless truth that you know a tree by its fruit. Unless you are willing to change first, don't bother trying to start a movement or change the world. Remember you are either under authority or in rebellion.

God always starts with you. The first step, like one star fish, begins with you. I know I would like Him to start with my wife, neighbors, church, or you for that matter, BUT He always starts at home, He starts with you. Then you are equipped to impart the blessings to your family, then your neighbors. God always works from the inside out. Religion has you do some outward task or discipline in hopes of changing inside. God changes your heart then everything else domino's in the right way. This is illustrated over and over in the Bible. Look at Gideon, Abraham, Noah. **Peter was used to change the world but first Peter was changed.** It starts with you. God loves you! He created you! God is good all of the time (cheers, yay)!!! God has good things for you! Not one word of His

The Purple Pill

promises has failed! Praise the Lord! I know you're excited at His goodness and His plans for your life. He has plans to prosper you, not to harm you! Yes, it all starts with you. You are the apple of His eye. He has coded your DNA with a divine purpose, that once you discover it, will get you so excited about life you won't know how you lived before.

Now that we understand our actions are fruit of our beliefs. What do you believe? What do your actions demonstrate? I need to shift gears in order to help you progress in your sojourn with God. One action I would like to share is one that marries God's truth, my circumstance, my heart, and my actions. This grew over time and God adds to it regularly and is, without a doubt, one of the keys to accelerating my walk towards maturity and power.

A manifesto is a published declaration of the intentions, motives, or views of the issuer – that would be me. I thought I should start out with the definition of "Manifesto" to save you time looking it up like I did. In light of the battle I wake up every day and declare my intentions, motives, and truths that have shaped my life. I decided I should write them down. That turns it into a "Manifesto."

> "The mouth of the righteous is a fountain of life…"
> -Proverbs 10:11a

I must offer a word of caution or warning. I

know you remember the verses in 1st Corinthians 1:27 that says God chose the foolish things of the world to shame the wise; God chose the weak things of the world to shame the strong. This is so true and applicable to this chapter and to our life. A person with greed in their heart can confess "the blessing of the Lord brings wealth" all day long and never see any fruit. This is why the world does not understand the Bible. They read it, but don't understand that without faith it does no good. Do you remember in Luke 4 Jesus is teaching in the synagogue and the people were amazed because his message had authority. That is a great example of what I am trying to point out. Jesus didn't read anything that the teachers of the law didn't already have. He read it in faith. He read it without being double minded. He read it and the power in it was revealed. The warning here is this is not a formula. Nothing about God is ever a formula. This is about a relationship with God. The closer you get to Him the easier it is to declare His truth over your life in faith.

> "From the fruit of their mouth a person's stomach is filled;
> with the harvest of their lips they are satisfied.
> The tongue has the power of life and death,
> and those who love it will eat its fruit."
> - Proverbs 18:20-21

The passage above is one of the first I took notice of after I was born again. I remember thinking that even when I say, "have a nice day" to someone that there is more to it than just pleasantries. I marveled at the idea that our tongue has the power of life and death. The reason I marveled at it was I believed it. This was the beginning of my declaration and it has grown from there. The power comes from words being spoken in faith.

God spoke and created the heavens and the earth and all that is in them (Hebrews 11:3, John 1:3, Genesis 1:3). That is power. God spoke and what He said is what appeared. If you read Genesis chapter 1 you will find the phrase "God said" 10 times. One of those ten times was "Let's make man in our image" (Genesis 1:26). I have been created in God's image and so have you (Genesis 1:27 and Psalms 139:13). He bestowed on me the power to speak. Cows don't speak. Only human beings speak. I speak every day. The problem most encounter is they speak and then say, "see nothing changed – no power." I see this all of the time. I tell them, "If you say so."

Speak what you believe. If you are speaking to see then believe – you have a problem. You are out of order. God is all about order – seedtime THEN harvest (Genesis 8:22). In Mark 11:23 Jesus said to speak to the mountain and do not doubt in your heart, but believe what you say then it will happen. **Believe what you say.** We need to be sure we understand God's word is true no matter what I see with my eyes or feel with my senses or think with my peanut brain. His Word is powerful and effective. His word and your faith translated you from darkness to light. My paraphrase of Romans 10:9-10 is you believe what you say, "Jesus is Lord," and you are saved. You believe it because you know in your inmost parts and believe that Jesus came to earth as a man, died on the cross for our sins, and rose from the dead for our life. You then speak in faith "Jesus is Lord!"

This power is double edged and can cut both ways. My tongue possesses the power of life and death. The enemy is always at work to deceive us into using our tongue for his purpose - death. When I speak words of faith I reap life, but when I speak unbelief I reap the whirlwind. **The truth is, we speak what we believe.** Religion may try to train us to change the outside but that never changes what's in our heart. That is out of order. God works from the inside out by sowing His word in our heart.

Fruit is evidence of what type of tree or vine has been planted. The tree comes from a seed. A seed that has been planted in good soil and watered. The fruit in my life is what grows from the seeds I've been planting. Each word I utter is a spiritual seed that will grow and turn into a harvest if it is planted in good soil and nurtured. I am reaping a harvest of life because I sow words of life. You are reaping a harvest of what you have spoken in the past. Jesus shared the parable of the sower in Matthew 13. His word is seed. We must plant the seed (His word) on good soil. Remember the soil is our heart:

- Our heart can be hard – have no understanding.

The Purple Pill

- Our heart can be shallow – receive the word with joy but have no root. When difficulty and persecution comes they last only a short time.
- Our heart can be overcome with weeds – worries and cares of this world choke it.
- Our hearts can be good soil - we understand it and harvest a crop 30, 60, or 100-fold.

We see then that fruit is dependent on the seed and on our heart, the soil. This begs to talk a little further about our heart.

So many people hear the first part – that their words are seeds, but never catch where and how to plant those seeds. You see these people all the time. They are like walking talking scripture reciting machines. But they are dry and without power. Most have missed the fundamental truth of how important the soil of our heart is. His word will stand forever. Heaven and earth will pass away but His word will stand forever. His word created everything. His word became flesh in Jesus. Yet His word can be stopped by our worries and cares. Worry can choke His word. I'm describing our hearts. If you wonder why or how can God's word be so powerful yet be stunted by a lowly human heart I believe the answer is in how good God is. He loves us. He is never going to force Himself upon us. He wants to court us as His bride in hope that we're sparked to pursue the depths of Him and find love beyond our comprehension.

Our hearts play a critical role in our ability to

live a life of power and love. Talking about our hearts in James he reminds us that praise and cursing should not come out of the same mouth. Can fresh and salt water come from the same spring? Olives do not come from fig trees. He goes on in chapter 4 and tells us to submit to God and purify our hearts so we're not double minded. Purify your heart. He tells us to do that. He tells how to do it too. But it is our choice. God doesn't force his will on us.

> Remember in Deuteronomy "choose you this day blessings or curses, life or death. Choose life." Same God, same message.

Now that we're on the same page concerning our beliefs, words, and harvest we must discuss what we do with it.

The following is my daily (not religiously) declaration. Think of this as a mirror of some of the truths in God's word for you to gaze in daily with the specific purpose to see YOUR reflection. The Spirit will help point out the gaps between what we think and what is true and gently line us up in the process. I will refer to this often throughout while sharing insights, revelations, and encouragement. Every day I wake up and thank God for another beautiful day. I usually spend time reading and in fellowship with my best friend (Holy Spirit). Then at some point I begin to declare His truth over my life. I begin to plant and water seeds in the soil of my heart. I will open my notes on my iPad and read the following declaration out loud. I suggest you read the following out loud and highlight what the Spirit highlights for you. Use this, change it, add to it as your own:

I am [your name] and I declare:

Who I am
I love the lord with all my Heart, soul, and strength (Lk 10:27)
I am a child of the most high God (1 Jn 3:1)
As for me and my house we will serve the lord! (Joshua 24:15)
I dwell in the secret place of the most high. I rest in the shadow of the almighty (Ps 91:1)
He is my refuge, my fortress, my God in whom I trust. (Ps 91:2)
I am born again by the blood of Jesus (1 Pet 1:19-23)
God takes me into his confidence (Pr 3:32)
God is pleased to have all his fullness dwell in me (col 1:19)
I am an oracle of God (1 Pet 4:11)
The lord has done great things for me and I am filled with joy! (Ps 126:3)
He teaches me the way I should go, and He counsels and watches over me. (Ps 32:8)
God loves me and his unfailing love surrounds me! (1 Jn 4:16 and Jn 3:16 and Ps 32:10)
The same spirit that raised Christ from the dead lives in me! (Ro 8:11)
Christ lives in me, the hope of glory (col 1:27)
God almighty beautifies, dignifies and crowns me with loving-kindness and tender mercy (Ps 103:4)
The Lord guides me always, satisfies my

needs, and strengthens my frame. I am like a well-watered garden, like a spring whose waters never fail!!! (Is 58:11)
I bring living water to dry ground, wherever I go life springs up (Is 44:3-4, Jn 4, Jn 14:12)
I am a minister of reconciliation (2 Cor 5:18)
I bring good news (Mt 4:23 and Mk 16:15)
I know all things (1 Jn 2:20)
I Hear counsel, receive instruction, and accept correction, that I may be wise in the time to come. (Pr 19:20)
I am crowned with knowledge (Pr 14:18)
My wife is beautiful, she's wise, understanding, and Prudent - a gift from the Lord! (Pr 19:14)

Healing
I am Healed by the stripes of Jesus (1 Pet 2:24 and is 53:5)
I bless the Lord and forget not all his benefits (Ps 103:2)
He Heals all my diseases and redeems my life from the pit (Ps 103:3-4)
Jehovah Rapha, the Lord that Heals me, lives in me (Ex 15:26 Ro 8:11)
He sent his word and Healed me (Ps 107:20)
His word is life and Health to my whole body! (Pr 4:22)
My tongue is a tree of life and brings healing. (Pr 15:4)
I lay hands on the sick and they recover (Mk 16:18)
I trust in the Lord with all my heart and lean not on my own understanding, in all my ways I acknowledge him and He makes my paths straight, I am not wise in my own eyes, I fear

the Lord and shun evil. This brings health to my body and nourishment to my bones. (Pr 3:5-8)

Prosperity
I honor the Lord with my wealth, with the first fruits of all my crops, then my barns are filled to overflowing and my vats brim over with new wine! (Pr 3:9-10)
God has plans to prosper me, to give me hope and a good future (Jer 29:11)
God gives sinners the task of gathering and storing up wealth to hand it over to me, the man of faith. (Ecc 2:26)
God bestows favor and honor on me and withholds no good thing from me (Ps 84:11)
I magnify the Lord and He takes pleasure in my prosperity (Ps 35:27)
God gives me the power to create wealth to establish his covenant on the earth (Dt 8:18)
I am blessed when I come in and I am blessed when I go out (Dt 28:6)
His blessing brings wealth and He adds no trouble to it. (Pr 10:22)
The Lord grants me abundant prosperity (Dt 28:11 and Pr 21:21)
I will lend to many but will borrow from none. (Dt 28:12c)
Everything I put my hand to prospers (Dt 28:8)
God brings increase to me and my children (Ps 115:14 and Gen 1:28)
My children will be mighty in the land (Ps 112:2)
I train my children in the way they should go and they never turn from it (Pr 22:6)

All of his blessings will chase me down and overtake me (Dt 28:2)
His favor is a shield about me (Ps 5:12)
He supplies all my needs according to his riches (Phil 4:19)
I am an oak of righteousness planted by the Lord, my leaf does not wither, whatever I do prospers (Is 61:4. Ps 1:3)

Authority
I am a man under authority (Mt 8:9, 1 Pet 2:13)
I have been given authority over all the power of darkness. (Eph 1:21 and 2:6 Mk 16:17)
I am seated with Christ in the Heavenlies far above all rule, power, and dominion (Eph 2:6)
I am anointed, have his seal of ownership; His Spirit in me (2 Cor 1:21-22)
The Spirit of the Lord is upon me; to bring good news of his Kingdom, proclaim freedom for the captives, the blind see, the deaf hear, the lame walk, this is the year of the Lord's favor (Lk 4:18-19)

Righteousness
I am the righteousness of God in Christ Jesus (2 Cor 5:21)
I am dead to sin (Ro 6:11,14 and 1 Pet 2:24)
I am alive to righteousness (1 Pet 2:24)
I have the mind of Christ! (1 Cor 2:16)

Divine Protection
No harm, will come near me, my family, or my dwellings (Pr 12:21)
His angels watch over me and carry out his

word (Ps 103:20)
God is my Help, my shield, and my very great reward! (Ps 115:11, 1 Pet 1:5, Gen 15:1)
I will never be shaken and I have no fear (Ps 112:6, 8, and Is 54:14)
God has victory in store for me, and He guards my course and protects my way (Pr 2:8)
No weapon forged against me will prosper. (Is 54:17)
I will refute every tongue that accuses me. (Is 54:17)
An enemy may come at me in one direction but He will flee from me in seven directions. (Dt 28:7)
God has victory in store for me. (Pr 2:7)
My steps are not hampered and my foot is not snared (Pr 4:12 and 3:26)

Faith
I live by faith in the son of God. (Gal 2:20)
I do not merely listen to the word, and deceive myself, I do what it says!!! (Ja 1:22)
I believe and therefore I speak (2 Cor 4:13)
My tongue has the power of life and death and I speak life! (Pr 18:21)
His word is truth (Jn 17:17)
His word is eternal (Mt 24:35)
What I see in the physical is temporary (2 Cor 4:18)
I walk by faith not by sight (2 Cor 5:7)
I am sure of what I hope for and certain of what I do not see. (Heb 11:1)
God gives life to the dead and calls things that are not as though they were! (Ro 4:17)

I am a believer (Mk 16:17)
All of his promises are yes for me and I speak the amen for his glory (2 Cor 1:20)
Every word of God contains the power to be fulfilled! (Lk 1:37)
My Heart is good soil and his word produces a crop of a hundredfold! (Lk 8:15)
I have been set free from the law of sin and death
I live by the law of the spirit of life (Ro 8:2)

Wisdom
God gives me wisdom and from his mouth comes knowledge and understanding (Pr 2:6)
He gives me wisdom, knowledge and joy. (Ecc 2:26)
Wisdom sets a garland of grace on my head and presents me with a crown of splendor (Pr 4:9)
Wisdom is my sister and understanding my kinsman. (Pr 7:4)
Wisdom speaks what is true (Pr 8:7)
Wisdom is more precious than rubies nothing I desire can compare with Her! (Pr 8:11)
Wisdom has understanding and power, riches, honor, enduring wealth, and prosperity (Pr 8:14 8:18)
She bestows wealth on those who love Her, making their treasuries full. (Pr 8:21)
Wisdom is supreme; therefore, I get wisdom! (Pr 4:7)

I am filled with the holy spirit (Acts 2:4 and 13:52)
The same spirit that raised Christ from the dead lives in me (Ro 8:11)

All the fullness of Christ lives in my flesh.
(Col 2:10)
God gives me wisdom and revelation to know
him and his incomparably great power!!!!
(Eph 1:17-19)
I have the ever-increasing fruit of the spirit;
love, joy, peace, patience, kindness, goodness,
faithfulness, gentleness, and self-control.
(Gal 5:22-25)
I have his peace and follow the path of peace
(Jn 14:27 and Col 3:15)

He took my sin and gave me his
righteousness (1 Pet 2:24)
He took my sickness and gave me Health (1
Pet 2:24)
He took my poverty and gave me prosperity
(2 Cor 8:9)
He took death and gave me life and life in
abundance!

God is good, all of the time!!! (Ro 12:2)
For not one word of his promises has failed!
(1 Kings 8:56)
Praise the Lord, praise His holy name, thank
you Father for all of your blessings!!! (Eph
1:3)

    Quite a declaration, isn't it? It takes about ten minutes. Boy it is amazing how much ten minutes a day can change your life. Your whole mindset is renewed to His truth. Your spirit is alive with the good things of God coming your way. Whenever I run across a great promise or truth in God's word I try to personalize it and add it to my declaration. God used Charles

Capps to encourage me to start speaking truth over my life. The world would describe this as how to think positive or maintain optimism. Even the world has realized there's power in words and a personal confession.

As we take action by speaking what we believe, by speaking His word in faith, be ready for the Holy Spirit to meet you as the words come out of your mouth. You may hear Him ask, "Do you really believe that?" You, like me, will stop right in the middle of it as He reveals gaps between what you say you believe and what you say by your actions. Just like me with my neighbor. He continues to peel the layers of our heart and share with us what He sees. **This sets you free and softens your heart to hear Him. He is answering your prayers with good things.** Our words are seeds, and within every seed is a harvest. When we say words, and act contrary we are planting seeds and immediately digging them up. We are limiting what God has for us. Words backed by action are evidence of living by faith. This brings the harvest. You are eating from what you have planted in the past. If you don't like the taste then you should change what you're sowing. We need to plant His seed and nurture it. He will bring increase (Psalms 115) and harvest - you will be blessed and find life abundantly.

Prayer

"Heavenly Father, forgive me for any and all times I have dug up your seeds of life. Help me

Lord to plant your seed in good soil of my heart. Help me water those seeds with your Spirit and my actions. Thank you for an abundant harvest of life and all of your blessings. Give me wisdom and discernment to steward everything you've given me that I might bring you glory and live in your perfect, good, pleasing will.

In the mighty name of Jesus, I pray, Amen!"

Six

The Invisible Wall

"LESSONS in life will be repeated until they are learned."
-Frank Sonnenburg

Reader's Digest published a funny story by Robert Alvarez about a father driving with his teenage daughter.

She asks, "Dad, do you know what the most commonly used letter in a girl's name is?"

The father replies, "Hmmm, is it a consonant or a vowel?

Silence.

He says, "Please tell me you know what consonants and vowels are."

The daughter rolls her eyes, "You're no fun, Dad. Forget it."

A few moments later he says, "What is a vowel?"

Daughter, "Ok, Ok. OK! A vowel is ... ahh ... eh ... well, oh ... uh ..."

The Invisible Wall

"Close enough," the father replies.

The girl in the story probably wants to get out of the car. Avoid talking about it. Change the subject. Any of those may work temporarily, but there is a lesson in each uncomfortable circumstance. James Allen said, **"In spite of popular belief Circumstance does not make a man; it reveals him to himself."** I love that quote. It shows the subtle yet critical difference between how people view circumstances. Most people think circumstances are the fences of life, when they run into one then they turn and go along with it. All the time wishing, thinking, even praying the circumstance will change. The wise ones realize the circumstances they are faced with are revealing who they are and, this is critical, what needs to change in them. You change for two reasons. Either you learn enough that you want to, or you've been hurt enough that you have to.

Let me explain. Life is like you are jogging along just fine then WHAM!! A circumstance, like an invisible wall, stops you cold. There you are laying on the ground holding a bloody nose wondering, "What just happened???" I am glad you asked, **you have just run into an invisible wall.** A circumstance that is screaming at you to change, unfortunately most people don't hear that. Most people feel pain and just want it to stop. They never hear anything. Like the girl being asked what a vowel is, she just wants out of the car. We just want to get away from the pain. This is a perfectly natural reaction. The thing to remember is God is not natural, He is

The Purple Pill

SUPERNATURAL and so are you because He lives in you. I want to lay out for you the principles you are caught in the middle of and what your supernatural reaction is. Do you remember when Jesus said that you will have trouble in this world, but take heart because He has overcome the world? Well, congratulations you are a living epistle of the Lord Jesus Christ. That invisible wall is trouble, but fear not for we know that God uses all things for the good of those who love Him and are called according to His purpose (Romans 8:28).

Did you get that last part, "called according to His purpose." His purpose. The natural reaction is to avoid pain, avoid trouble and there honestly isn't anything wrong with that as long as you are fulfilling God's purpose. You were called for His purpose which is your blessing. If your purpose is on the other side of that invisible wall then you better not walk off in a different direction. Most people do. They follow the path of least resistance and they find themselves in a dry and weary land where there is no water, but there is lots of company!

> When you know His purpose for you, then you know there is no obstacle, wall, or circumstance that can stop you.

This is your supernatural reaction - get over it, through it, or around it. You are no longer being conformed but you are being transformed by the renewal of your mind so you can test and approve what God's will, or purpose, is. His good, pleasing, and perfect will. God's will is on the other side of that invisible wall. You cannot stop. You certainly can't go the other direction. You will be miserable no matter how many cars, kids, or houses you have. Your life is in Him! His will is perfect, what He wants for you is better than you can hope, think, or imagine!!!

   THAT WALL IS A TEST YOU WERE BORN TO PASS!

   The living God always works from the inside out. He begins with our heart first. Normally, we want Him to change our circumstances, all of the outward things we continually face. When our heart is completely His, things begin to change externally. We will discuss how you uncover His divine purpose for your life in following chapters. Right now, we have to continue to talk about these trials and tests that we find in life.

   There are examples of this throughout the Bible and in our lives. Abraham, Joseph, Moses, and David are just a few. The prophet Samuel anoints David as the next king of Israel (1 Samuel 16). Now he is alone in the hills watching over his father's sheep. We know that while he was watching his father's sheep he killed the lion and the bear. Now, what I am about to say is not found in scripture, I want to be clear on that. This is my imagination based on the facts from scripture. Putting myself in his shoes I can imagine the biggest challenge David faced was the loneliness and monotony of each day. He began to pour out his heart to God.

The Purple Pill

He would pray for his brothers in battle, he'd pray for his family, and their herds. He would also think and pray about growing up. Prayer always brought comfort and eased his loneliness.

One evening, at dusk, David noticed the herd moving about and not settling down for the night. It was not normal. He couldn't see anything wrong, but his adrenaline began to rise. His senses were on full alert as he picked up his staff and left his campfire to get a closer look. He could hear his heart pounding and his breathing seamed so loud. "Settle down David, settle down. Think, Look, Listen," he thought. Suddenly he heard the bleats of fear off to his right. He looked and the sheep were running. He scanned intently through the fading light. He caught a glimpse of movement. It wasn't a sheep, it was moving too smoothly. Sheep would bounce more as they moved. It was a LION! It was carrying a sheep in its mouth. Immediately David ran towards the lion. The lion stopped to face David. Running right at it David struck the lion with his whole heart and all of his strength. He killed it in one mighty blow! An intense rush of emotion rose up; victory, joy, and peace almost indescribable washed over him. David whispered, "Thank you God."

Well, that is my imagination and adaptation of the story of the shepherd boy David found in 1 Samuel 16 and 17. I am amazed every time I think about David. It is not normal to run at a lion. It's not. He did the same thing when a bear came. He ran at the bear with a stick! I hope you're hearing what I'm saying. Think about that. It's human nature to run from danger, not towards it. Do you think he killed the first lion that showed up? We don't know since the Bible doesn't say. I can imagine if I was there the first lion attack would scare me to death and I would probably run away. I would run away from the test until I knew and believed in my heart that God's will was on the other side of me killing that lion. I don't know if I would kill him the second, or third time, but I know at some point I would figure out I need to kill that lion and by the grace of God I would, just like David did. Then when the bear showed up - been there done that - dead bear!

Now let's look at how David did it. I think this is the best part. The bible says the Spirit of the Lord rested on David (1 Samuel 16:13). I believe this helps explain why he thought so differently from most people. This is why he thought with a heart of faith. **You see God plus a young man's heart will defeat any adversary.** The critical part here is the young man believes God. He must see the lion as a test of his faith, not a day to die. I can sense hope rising in your heart as you understand and confirm that the "how" is not dependent on your strength. David didn't have to be stronger, faster, or more ferocious than a lion. He just needed to believe then God made a way. It is evidence of faith. To fulfill our destiny, we must know God has more. Better things are yet to come. Bigger tests are also yet to come as our faith grows.

In Matthew 4 Jesus said, "Worship the Lord your God, and serve Him only." He was

The Purple Pill

responding to Satan after being shown all the kingdoms of the world and their authority. Satan's offer came with a catch – worship him. The average Christian, maybe even the average person, has figured out you worship God and you do not worship Satan. It seems almost too obvious, too simple. Everyone knows that. Is that really a temptation or a test? Jesus passed it. My question is have you?

"Yes," flies out of our mouths like a reflex. I know. Over and over. I know that – worship God. I began to slow down and listen to the Holy Spirit. You know Him. The still quiet voice inside your heart. He's the one telling you that you may not know everything and He wants to help you. Revelation can only come when you're open to Him and understand that there is more in each one of His words than you understand right now. He desires to reveal himself to you but you must seek Him.

As I opened myself to His leading and began asking for more. He showed me the test was a short cut. You see Jesus came to bring His kingdom to earth. He introduced the Kingdom of God and then entrusted us to complete His work. The devil offered him a shortcut to get the job done. I started to reflect and think about how many times I'm offered and/or take a shortcut. The Holy Spirit reminds me of Adam and Eve eating the fruit, Abram with Ishmael, Moses at the waters of Meribah, Saul at Gilgal.

In the garden of Eden sin entered the world because Adam and Eve saw with their eyes that

The Invisible Wall

it looked pleasing and believed God was withholding a blessing from them. That is always a lie. Satan still uses it constantly. The short cut was to eat and not believe God. The short cut brought death.

God promised Abram that his offspring would be like the stars of the sky and the sand of seashore. Abram saw his barren wife. Time went by. His wife offered him a short cut by sleeping with her maidservant. The shortcut resulted in Ishmael the patriarch of Islam.

Dying in the desert from lack of water the Israelites cried out to Moses. God told him to speak to the rock and water would flow for them and their animals. Moses did not speak to the rock, instead he struck it with his staff like he had done before. **God is not trying to teach us a formula for success, He is trying to teach us obedience is success, because he tells us only what is best for us**. The shortcut resulted in Moses not being able to lead the Israelites into the promised land.

God told Saul to wait at Gilgal for Samuel to offer a sacrifice for the Lord's favor. He thought Samuel wasn't coming so he would do it. He did do what God said, just not in order according to His instructions. He took a short cut. Samuel was to offer the sacrifice for Saul. The result of this shortcut was Saul's kingdom did not endure. God then anointed David as king of Israel and his house was on the throne forever. That is the family line Jesus came from.

The Purple Pill

A short cut is the way out that appeals to our natural nature, but is fundamentally wrong because you are putting yourself and your thinking above God. Remember we are supposed to serve Him only. **A short cut tests if we believe what we say. Because your actions show what you believe.** This isn't just a question of sinning, or falling short of the mark. This is a question of who or what is on the throne of your heart. This is a question of who you are serving. Remember the call for your whole heart. Jesus told us to love the Lord our God with all of our heart. Proverbs 3 says trust in the Lord with all of your heart. We would just say, "trust in the Lord." God adds with "all of your heart." Why do you suppose He added that? Because He knows what's in a man. You can talk about sanctification but at some point it has to be more than christianese (or church talk). Sanctification is a real work of the Holy Spirit in your life. It is for your whole heart.

The tests we run into are walls or obstacles along our path of destiny. These tests reveal our heart to us, not to God. He knows what's in your heart. He needs you to see it. Here are a couple scriptures to think about:

> "For you, O God, tested us; you refined us like silver."
> - Psalms 66:10

> "The crucible for silver and the furnace for gold, but the Lord tests the heart."
> - Proverbs 17:3

The Invisible Wall

My wife and I are raising four kids that still very young. It is amusing when we ask if they brushed their teeth. My son quickly blurts out "yes!" Being a father that has ears and can hear when his electric toothbrush is running I ask again. This may happen two or three times before my son realizes that he is only lying to himself and he sheepishly goes and brushes his teeth. There is something about our fallen nature that tells us if you don't know my flaws then I can get away with them or I have no need to address them. This is far from the truth, in fact it is false. But we must see our heart in light of the test, for it is then that we may choose, by His grace, to change. Praise God for His loving-kindness and patience!

Think about the things we discussed earlier in chapter two, The Mirror. Could those things be tests and the very things God is using to help us fulfill our destiny? Is it possible we just have not recognized it and, taking faith into our own hands, flit off to another place hoping to avoid pain and find better pasture. Often crying out to God to change everything outside of us, when all He cares about is setting you free by changing you and not what surrounds you. In Psalms 23 God is preparing a table for you in the presence of your enemies. Problems weren't vanquished, God worked in the midst of them. I propose the whole time we should only ask God where He would like us to be and go there. He will use everything there for the good, including you.

The Purple Pill

Prayer
"Father in Heaven, thank you for your loving-kindness. Thank you for watching over your word that it never returns void, but always accomplishes what you sent it for. Thank you for declaring I am set apart, holy, and useful to do your will. Help me Lord see my heart the way you see it. Help me pass the tests, fight the good fight, and bring you glory.
In Jesus name, Amen."

Seven

The Maze

> "WHEN written in Chinese the word 'crisis' is composed of two characters, one represents danger and the other represents opportunity."
> - John F. Kennedy

We get saved, when we confess with our mouth "Jesus is Lord," and we believe in our heart that God raised Him from the dead. We then begin a journey where our heart is being transformed. Our spirit is sealed at that moment by the Holy Spirit. Our soul or our mind is still seeing, tasting, hearing, feeling everything the body or our flesh is sending to it. Our soul is also hearing from our born-again spirit. Our spirit is hearing Him, the Truth.

A hardened heart makes it very difficult to hear His voice. A hardened heart comes about through our daily routine of what we're basting our heart in. If we throw our heart in the salt spring of the world we find, over time our heart gets sour and hard, like leather being boiled and then dried. In fact, in olden days this is how they would make armor.

Remember the Holy Spirit has sealed your spirit inside your heart. The Holy Spirit is actually living water (John 7:38). Living water which transforms that sour hard shell back into a supple heart of flesh. The problem is you can't have both. You cannot have fresh and salt water flow from the same spring.

The trap in this is the daily routine that is developed. We try to avoid the trap by imitating what's worked before or follow someone else's directions to avoid the invisible walls. This sounds like a great idea and it would be except the invisible walls are actually part of a maze and each person's path is different. We think a routine or discipline will keep us safe from the enemy's trap. In reality, it is part of the trap, a detour from God's best for you. I love routine and discipline but do not ever let those things rule over relationship. Relationship keeps us from blindly wearing a rut. There is only one way to navigate this invisible maze we call life and that's listening to the only one who sees it, loves us, and longs to spend time with us.

This trap is dangerous but it is also an opportunity. Socrates, the renown philosopher who lived about 400 years before Christ, said, "Beware the barrenness of a busy life." The routine is what forms your thoughts and

The Purple Pill

attitudes. The thoughts and attitudes make up who you are and what you do. That is why you wear the clothes that you do, that is why you live where you live. Your thoughts lead to your actions. I like to say that your actions are servants of your thoughts. In the movie "Tomorrow Land" the main character made a statement worth remembering, "There are two wolves and they are always fighting. One is darkness and despair. The other is light and hope. Which wolf wins?" The answer is the one you feed. The truth here is do you feed your mind with the twisted half-truths of the world or do you feed your mind the absolute truth of God's word.

Worship demonstrates who is on the throne of your heart. To say it differently **worship is your daily routine demonstrating what rules your heart**. Good or bad, light or dark, God or you. Does His word rule or do worldly circumstances? Does His word reign or does the world's wisdom guide? My simple daily choices loudly proclaim who is on the throne of my heart.

Those who let money make their decisions demonstrate a life that proves one cannot serve both God and money. Greed destroys because it abuses the fundamental purpose for which prosperity and wealth were created for. Tithes and offerings are not about money. God wants you to see your heart. Your giving is evidence of what you believe. God's desire is for you to be free, not bound by the ways of the world. Give and it will be given to you, a good measure pressed down and overflowing, will be poured into your lap. If you give and are not walking in His abundance then there is heart problem not a God problem. Who or what is on the throne of your heart?

Those who want to believe most of the time but would like themselves to remain on the throne sometimes or at least for important decisions, demonstrate a life with an appearance of godliness but lacking in power. For instance, a person who goes to church, may even tithe, and then goes home and acts like everyone else in the world - soaking their heart in the mindless chatter of the world and renewing their mind with worldly wisdom. This, honestly, describes a majority of Christians. We then wonder why our lives seems void of the power we hear of in the Bible and hope God will do something. This is also why the world laughs at the church. People can smell a hypocrite from a quite some distance. I am not asking who appears to be on the throne of your heart when you are at church. To navigate this invisible maze, we must listen to the Master. I am asking who is on the throne of your heart when nobody is watching.

> Those who worship in spirit and in truth are simply obedient to God. He is on the throne of their heart.

David was described as a man after God's own heart. He ran nose first into one invisible wall after another. Read 1 Samuel 30. David had been anointed king of Israel yet Saul was still king. David was running with about 600 men from Saul and had been for years. David seeking rest from the relentless pursuit of Saul goes to the Philistines, his enemies, for rest. Achish, king of the Philistines, gives him a town to stay in called Ziklag. After a short season of living there one day David and his men are returning to Ziklag at the direction of the Philistine King and they find their homes burned, and all of their wives, children, and animals are gone - taken captive. Talk about a bloody nose, concussion, and bewilderment - what happened? Pause and reflect on what David did. David inquired of the Lord, "Should I pursue them?" THINK ABOUT THAT. David asked, "Should I pursue them?" Most men faced with a similar situation would never even consider asking God what to do – they would act first and ask God to bless them on the way.

Just imagine the shock of arriving home to a pile of smoldering ruins and your family kidnapped! Your mind is racing to process and you are certain of the culprits. As for me I would begin charging like a rabid hyena - the anger and rage overtaking me! I would act worse when I caught them. Not David. **Think about this.** He had been anointed by Samuel as King of Israel around 15 years earlier. Years waiting in faith, trusting in God. Years! I would be fighting a little confusion. God, you said I was king and now it's been years? Did I hear you right, did you change your mind? Not David, the man after God's own heart, he believed. He trusted and believed so much that even with 600 faithful men at their wits end ready to stone him to death, David still asks God, "Should I pursue them?" God says yes. They catch them and get everything back – they lost no one. This is the same time Saul decides to talk to the witch of Endor then is wounded in battle and killed. In 24 hours David went from the biggest test of his life to being enthroned King of Israel. David has always had a descendant on the throne. David worshipped in spirit and in truth, simply being obedient to God. He had placed Jehovah-Raah, the Lord his Shepherd, on the throne of his heart.

In Genesis 22:5 Abram said to his servants, "Stay here with the donkey while I and the boy go over there. We will worship and then we will come back to you." You see God told Abram to sacrifice his one and only son, Isaac. Think about this - Abram saw the wall coming and kept running full speed! Abram did or was doing what God told him to do. I have to point out his words of faith. You see that he said, "we will go and we will come back." He had faith in God. He believed even if he had to sacrifice his son that God would raise him from the dead to fulfill His promise to Abram, made years earlier, that He would bless him and his descendants would be more than the stars in the sky. Abram had vacated the throne of his heart and yielded to Jehovah Jireh, the Lord his Provider!

I pray you hear the Holy Spirit gently, lovingly, kindly, graciously asking, "Who is on the throne of your heart?" He is calling people from the dry and weary place they've settled to His living water where you will never thirst again. Invite Him onto the throne, trusting in faith that He desires better for you and your whole family than you can even hope or imagination. Take this leap and you'll know the feeling Peter had when he first stepped out of the boat then you will see the all-powerful, always loving, Savior look you in the eyes of the heart and say, "follow me." Your life will never be the same. With the Holy Spirit on the throne of your heart you will experience power, love, and miracles even greater than what Jesus did. God is good, all of the time. When the enemy comes and tempts your mortal body with a shortcut, or an easy way out, then you will say like Jesus, "Worship the Lord your God, and serve Him only."

God tests us to show us our hearts. He is producing the character of His Son in you.

A revelation is God revealing truth about Himself (His Word) that you previously had not understood. I believe every time you get a revelation then a test follows. In Matthew 16 Peter is given the revelation that Jesus is the Messiah, the son of the living God. Awesome, earth shattering revelation!! Let's celebrate! Jesus tells him this was revealed by His Father in heaven, then goes on to tell the disciples that he will be betrayed, killed, and raised to life. Peter pulls him aside to rebuke him, "Never Lord!" Jesus says, "Get behind me Satan, you do not have in mind the concerns of God, but merely human concerns."

Notice how he understands the scripture. He is blessed with revelation. Then he instantly runs into an invisible wall. That wall was a test of his beliefs. God wants to set you free. The process He uses is to test what you say you believe. Anyone can say anything. **The ones who believe what they say show it by their actions.**

Peter figures out by revelation that Jesus is the messiah. The MESSIAH then tells him he will be betrayed, killed, and raised to life. The MESSIAH told him that. Get it. One revelation to another, but something went terribly wrong. Peter didn't believe Jesus and proved it by his actions. If Peter rightly and truly believed Jesus was the Messiah wouldn't he believe everything he said? Instead it didn't line up with what Peter already believed about the Messiah. Peter showed that his beliefs trumped God's by his actions.

God is in process of showing Peter his heart. He is showing Peter what he believes. This is the only way Peter, in light of the truth, can ever be set free. God does the same with us. We say what we believe and then we run into an invisible wall. It is just a hurdle. Are you going to act or react according to your old way of thinking or according to the truth that you say you believe?

Here is the easiest example of all. Giving. God doesn't need your money. Ps 50:12b says, "...the world is mine, and all that is in it." All that is in the world is His. Why does he ask you to give? You know Luke 6:38, "give and it will be given to you...." Malachi 3:10, "Bring the whole tithe...." Luke 6:30, "Give to everyone who asks...." 2 Corinthians 9:6-8, "Remember this: Whoever sows sparingly will also reap sparingly, and whoever sows generously will also reap generously. Each of you should give what you have decided in your heart to give, not reluctantly or under compulsion, for God loves a cheerful giver. And God is able to bless you abundantly, so that in all things at all times, having all that you need, you will abound in every good work."

I watch born again Christians struggle with this all the time. They say, "well tithing is not in the new testament." That's true, it was introduced by Abraham before the Law of Moses (Genesis 14). The same people love to remind themselves that they are Abraham's children according to Galatians 3 and have all the blessings he had. There is always room to justify your beliefs over God's word. It doesn't validate your belief.

So, why does God ask you to give if He doesn't need your money? He wants to show you your heart. God loves a cheerful giver because a cheerful giver believes God. A cheerful giver believes that when they give God will give back and they don't have to worry. Religion has people give out of obligation and peer pressure. God doesn't want you to give a dime if you're not believing and cheerful.

PAIN

Every test may result in discomfort to our selfish nature or carnal nature - most people call this pain. An athlete beats his body in training so as to compete to win the race. The body screams but the spirit leads. The teacher is always quiet during the test. The teacher cannot pass the test for you or you won't grow in your understanding, confidence, or calling in life. The enemy comes with thoughts that God's will shouldn't cause pain. This is a lie. Throughout His word we read that God tests our hearts. Our faith will be tested. In fact, Jesus said you will have trouble in this world, but take heart for He has overcome the world.

> In the midst of a test we experience pain, silence, and confusion - these always come before victory!

Pain from our flesh, silence from our Teacher, confusion from our enemy. You will pass the test by doing what you were taught in spite of what it "feels" like and in spite of the enemy's lies, and do it over and over again building a routine of faithfulness. Think about a baby chick developing inside the egg. If someone cracks the egg open, rather than letting the chick struggle as it cracks its way out, then the chick actually is not strong enough to live. The struggle breaking its way out is what strengthens it to live outside the shell or you could say to live its destiny. Your struggles are the very thing that you need to strengthen you for life ahead. That life ahead is good. Struggles last only a short

The Purple Pill

time.

God has a great plan for you. He wants to prosper you and use you to be a blessing everywhere you go. To do that you must believe Him. You must trust Him and grow in Him. You must see your purpose is through the test opposing you, THEN you will stand up like David and say, "who dares come against the living God's anointed?" That is who you are – you are God's anointed. Your passion burns as you take hold of the truth.

> His Kingdom come, His will be done

God is doing a work that will shape eternity. **He is calling you to play your part.** Your flesh may scream but your spirit will drive you to the bosom of your Creator, your loving Father, and everything He has for you.

You have been designed for this moment and His purpose. Deep calls to deep. The Spirit is calling you even as I speak. I will close this chapter with a question for you to ponder in your heart.

> Are you willing to pursue His purpose for your life in spite of temporary pain and find intimate relationship with your Creator?

Tell Him in prayer and show Him in actions.

Prayer
"Father in heaven, here I am. I am yours. I

am willing. I want to pursue your purpose for my life. I know you love me and your plans are perfect. I want everything you have for me. Help me act in line with your Spirit's leading. I love you.

In Jesus name, Amen."

Eight

The Process

YOUR Response to the Test

In school, we learn lessons before the test, in life, we take the test before we learn the lesson.

My Garden

On an early summer morning watering my lawn, the sun began peeking out of the East. This is my favorite time of the day, watching the morning wake listening to the sounds of our creek. I have found this is when my best friend, the Holy Spirit, speaks with me. This is my "garden." So, there I am recounting how hard it has been over the last year but especially the last couple months. I had run into another invisible wall the night before. I know God is showing me my heart. I have checked my

The Process

actions over and over to ensure they line up with my words and what I believe. It shouldn't be this hard - what is going on? Is this the biggest test of all? I pray, "Spirit why has it been so hard?" I hear him as clearly as I hear these words in my mind. He says, "Rob, you need to change the way you think."

I need to change the way I think? I teach people how to change the way they think! I have changed the way I think? Again, I hear, "You need to change the way you think." I think to myself, "I need to change the way I think...? Hmmmmm." Again, "**You** need to change the way **you** think." This time when He speaks, what I hear and understand all in a blink of an eye is this: "Rob, you need to change the way you think because I cannot give you what you have asked me for if you continue to limit me by your thinking. You HAVE TO CHANGE THE WAY YOU THINK for me to answer your request, and to fulfill your heart's desire. The reason it has been so hard is you are doing things I have not asked you to do. You are doing things I have asked your wife to do. Do what I ask and it will be easy. Rob, you can know everything there is about building a skyscraper. You can have all the knowledge about the foundation, concrete, structural steel, permits, and licenses. But you will **never** build a skyscraper **by yourself**. I use people." God has just jerked me out of a rut. The funny thing about ruts is they are really comfortable but exhilaration, joy, and laughter overflow when you get out of one.

I stand there watering the grass and a huge

The Purple Pill

smile breaks over my countenance. God almighty whispered directly to me! I heard him! I NEED TO CHANGE THE WAY I THINK. I need to put my hand to what He has asked and not to everything that is in front of me. I need to let others do what I know they can do and trust Him. I am excited. I drop the hose to go tell my wife what I had just experienced. Excited I rush into the house and before I can say a word she says, "Stop! I have to tell you this. I have known this for a month and haven't said it. I don't want to step on your toes. I don't want to hurt you, but I keep feeling like God wants me to be in the front managing our business. You help me when I need it, then you can focus on the other things He has for us." I smile and grin and almost cry saying, "I know." Then I shared what God whispered to me. God is good! The blessings and ease that came to our business was evident in less than 36 hours. It was like heaven's gate opened and good things just happened and came to us.

> The Apostle Peter changed the world,
> but before he changed the world,
> Peter needed to change.

I began putting my hand to what He had put in my heart. I started writing and developing what God had given me to share with His bride – the Body of Christ. Over my life and especially the last few months God showed me His purpose for my life. That is what I had asked for and that is what He is in process of giving me. I was so narrow in focus I could not see. God turned my focus from me to Him and then I began to see His purpose for me here in this time and in this place. He's anointed me to bring living water to dry ground – everywhere I go life springs up. I was too busy doing other good things but not doing what He asked me to do. This book is evidence of what I put my hand to. I knew I had to share the message to help others if they need to change the way they think.

Let me step back and give you some background. This will be entertaining since you can read this knowing what God has already said and done to me. You see I help people learn from things that go wrong. For the last fifteen plus years I have been all over the nation teaching and leading people through investigations, coaching, and training to help them understand why unexpected painful events have happened. Every single time people see that there was wrong thinking that directly led to some catastrophe – small or big. Why the gas plant blew up, or why the flare overfilled, or why the car ran out of gas, or why the father missed a soccer game.

I learned, taught, and lived a process that helps you understand why things go wrong, what needs to change, and how to change it. I started off working with corporate America. The process is amazing. The more I learned, the more I taught, and the more **I changed**. What drew me to the process was the foundational, biblical truth that it was built on. Bob Nelms, Failsafe Network, developed the process in the mid 80's and I was fortunate enough to work

The Purple Pill

with him as an affiliate. Corporate America anxiously embraced the process. This was the Sermon on the Mount without the book and verse annotation. His truth works anywhere.

The most surprising thing I learned is that people knew about all of the problems that led to a huge failure. All of them! I've performed hundreds of investigations and worked on failures all over the world and I always found the same thing!!! Unresolved small problems cause big problems. We call it the conservation of wretchedness, but I will save the details for a later time. People always knew things weren't right but they didn't think it would ever kill someone or lead to a catastrophe. A quick example is a little water spot on the ceiling of your kitchen. No big deal, but if it is ignored you're not fixing a small leak on your roof now but you're replacing your roof later. Tearing out sheet rock. Fighting a mold problem. All of this because you did not act on a little water spot. If you ever thought or imagined the pain and money of a new roof, mold abatement, sheet rock, and paint then you would have fixed the roof immediately with a nail, new shingle, and a dab of paint. People do not connect the dots to "see" what's coming. This process enables people to "see" and understand.

I began to realize that this process and these truths are for anyone. You shouldn't have to wait for your roof to collapse, or something to blow up, or burn down to learn these freeing truths. I always worked in the background searching for ways to share this process in all arenas of life.

The Process

The value to learn this way of "seeing" before a marriage wobbles out of control, or before a bank starts to foreclose is priceless.

It's funny the better you know a subject the simpler it becomes. The better I learned how to perform formal failure investigations with evidence teams and stakeholder meetings, the simpler the process became. In fact, three elements stood out among the details and complexities of the process. The following is what I have learned to be the best way to respond to those invisible walls that jump up, knock you down, and leave you holding your nose.

Bias and Blame.

> "For since the creation of the world God's invisible qualities—his eternal power and divine nature—have been clearly seen, being understood from what has been made, so that people are without excuse."
> - Romans 1:20

In order to clearly see we cannot look through a skewed lens. Bias is like a kaleidoscope - it completely changes the true picture. In fact, bias blinds. **Blame and bias keep you from ever seeing the truth**. As long as your mind is made up (bias) before you investigate, then you are blind. When I would go to a site and form a team to investigate I knew my number one enemy was bias. That is why they brought an outsider in - to help them see and understand what happened. Blame goes hand in hand with bias. Whenever we can blame someone else then we shut off our mind and sidestep our responsibility. We don't have to change because it is not our problem. Step 1 is to renounce, turn away from bias and blame. You will never understand why anything happened unless you release blame. Remember Jesus said to forgive. He also said to take the plank out of your eye then you can see to take the speck out of your brother's. The plank is bias and blame. These are two of the enemy's favorite tactics to keep people in bondage and darkness. Blame, in biblical terms, is cursing. This is a significant reason people cannot seem to live the blessed life and struggle - taking one step forward then two steps back. The measure you use will be used for you and blame is cursing. This is not the life anyone wants but it explains the "two steps back" phenomenon. This is worthy of a future book in itself, let's just say we are called to bless. That means we are called to speak what God sees and He sees the original intent of good. Speak the truth in love. The truth is Jesus. The truth is what God says, not what you see. When we let what we see mold our thoughts then we are living by sight, not by faith. The bible describes thoughts that are built up against the knowledge of God (truth) as strongholds.

Evidence.

> The world looks for formulas. God looks for relationships.

The Process

Evidence is all around us. Immerse yourself in truth. Our enemy is bias. We have already made up our minds, in other words you can't see what is actually there – you only see what you think is there. Remember God said, "It is not good to be alone." God uses people. People see from a different perspective or you might say through a different lens. Other people see what you cannot see. People keep you honest. You know you will lie to yourself, right? Have you ever counted calories? I have. Remember, if it's true then other people will see the same thing, but if it isn't then you may certainly have an opportunity to change the way you think.

The Johari Window describes a person as being made up of primarily two parts: The "open" part above the horizontal line and the "hidden" part below the line (see figure below). When I meet someone, I have an "open" side that I show them, but I also have things that I conceal or hide. For example, if we met for the first time I would smile and shake your hand and talk about what I do, but I wouldn't share the heated family discussion I had earlier in the day or some weakness I struggle with. I would "hide" that. Sounds like Adam in the garden, doesn't it? I think I'm just fine going through life like that because I justify you don't need to know everything about me. Now of course the more time we spend together the more and more I will share. You can think of the "hidden" part shrinking, move the horizontal line down, and the "open" part is growing.

The Purple Pill

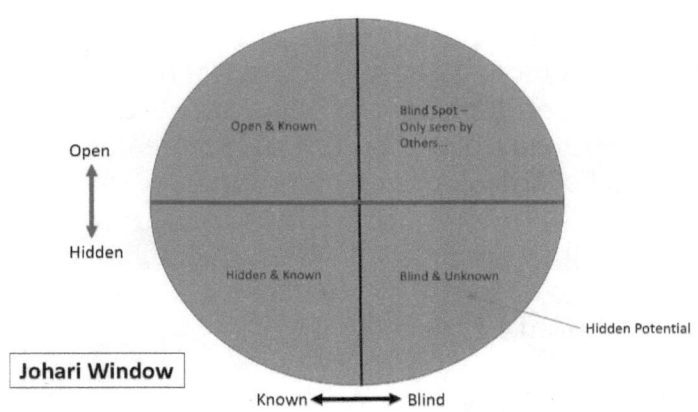

Actually, I am not ok living like this because All I see are the sections labeled "Open and Known" and "Hidden and Known." The vertical line separates what I see and what others are able to see. **I am blind to the part of me** represented as the area right of the vertical line. The open half, in this case, that I share with you, consists of what I see and my blind spots or what I don't see. You see what I'm blind to, but I do not. I see the "Hidden and Known" but not the "Blind and Unknown." No one sees the blind and unknown because I won't let them. This is the area of untapped potential which God calls out of you to fulfill your destiny. I can hear the wheels spinning in your head right now…, I need people to help me see what I cannot see. People I trust help me more because I show them more. Isn't that fascinating? The more I let people speak into my life, the more I listen to what people share that they see, which I am blind to, then the more I move the vertical line to the right, thus shrinking the "Blind and Unknown." The more I trust people, then the more I will let them see the real me. The horizontal line will move down, thus shrinking the "hidden" and "unknown" areas. The more I grow as a human being. The more I surrender and trust God with ALL I am then the more hidden potential is revealed! The key to all of this is honest relationship.

> "Faithful are the wounds of a friend; but the kisses of an enemy are deceitful."
> - Proverbs 27:6

If people don't know or like you then even when they see your blind spots they won't tell you. They will only share that if you have invited them to that level of relationship. You may see someone walking into Walmart with their makeup smeared and not say anything, but you would if it was your daughter.

The major point is that God uses people to help us see the truth. When we get together and look at the same evidence, sharing what we see, you will be amazed at the insight and understanding that is revealed through other's eyes. It is incredible.

Blessing and Cursing

In light of this insight into the way people compartmentalize themselves let's discuss the overflow of our heart and what comes out of our mouths. I lived a long time knowing I should bless and not curse. I have read scriptures about the tongue in James and Proverbs many times. I have worked really hard at not speaking curses. I'm sure you have too, and I think it's commendable. The huge change came for me in light of how I may have thoughts stirring in me but I won't speak them or share them. I thought that was good, and to a degree it is. When I have thoughts in my heart about people that are not good, not loving, and may not even be spoken then be assured I have not tapped into His thoughts. His thoughts are for your good. It is so easy to speak what we see or to think what we see is true. God isn't dreaming of people hurting themselves or others, He has dreams that are for your good. He is dreaming the bitter hurt person who hurts others will be set free and share His loving kindness. We are called to bless and not curse. This means we are called to speak what God's thinking about people, not what we may see. I realized those thoughts that I had managed or tried to manage to put a cork in are wrong. I don't want thoughts contrary to God's. The devil has thoughts contrary to God. I don't want to hide thoughts contrary either. This is a critical step in renewing your mind. I do not want to just cork a bitter well. There is no room for it. I cannot have clean and bitter water from the same well.

Now is the time for you to take note of the evidence that is around you. Allow others to see it too. Your job as you see people and their blind spots is to bless them. Speak what God sees, which is always good. Everyone has treasure in them. Ask God to help you see the treasure He knit into people around you. Anyone can walk in a room tell you it's too hot. That doesn't help you or them. The man who walks in a room that is too hot and lowers the temperature helps everyone. Don't be a thermometer, be a thermostat. Discuss what's happened, the invisible wall or problem, in light of what you see. The best evidence you can use is His word. His word speaks His thoughts, desires, and dreams for you. You will see the truth of His word manifest in your circumstances. The only thing to discuss is the evidence in light of the truth. Not opinions, not theories. Any step you take in understanding is supported by a foundation of evidence. It doesn't help to see your gaps without knowing and seeking His plans to fill those gaps and bring redemption and victory to your life.

Revelation

The final, and liberating, step is to look at yourself in light of the evidence. The answer you find to this question is shocking:

> What is it about the way I am that contributed to this?

When you honestly answer this and others confirm your revelation you will experience freedom to a greater degree than you've experienced before. You will feel like doing a back-flip. The end result of this exercise is you think differently. I have had Plant Managers walk through this process. At the beginning, they are sure they will find egregious incompetence. At the end, they stand up in front of everyone and confess they contributed to the failure because they knowingly allowed unsafe work for the sake of production! Trust me, those men are never the same. They have changed for the better because they think differently. Their subordinates see it. Their Executive Vice Presidents see it. Most importantly their wives and kids see it. I am talking about being pulled out of a fox hole they didn't even know they were in. Honestly, they smell the aroma of Christ and His Kingdom that is near.

What is very important here is how you see. In the kingdom of God, believing is seeing. Culture is the prevailing value system of a group of people. This is evidenced by politics, education, arts, athletics, and so on. Interestingly the word culture comes from the Latin word cultus which means worship. A cult worships their beliefs. **When we are out of order - worshiping our beliefs about God instead of worshiping God - something dies.** We no longer believe God, we only believe our beliefs about God - life is gone, leaving religion.

Do you recall (chapter 4) we have been blessed with sight, insight, and foresight? Most people see only with natural sight and make evaluations and judgments based only on the flesh. We are designed in the image of God:

We have a body, soul, and spirit and each part helps us "see." Our body has natural sight, our

The Process

soul has insight, and our spirit has foresight, although most people never tap into their spirit. The devastating part about this is that is where the Holy Spirit resides and talks to us. A majority of Christians think God doesn't talk to them but the truth is He is always talking, they just aren't tuned into Him. He is a Spirit and communicates with our spirits. Think of it from the inside out. At the core is your heart or spirit. Your soul or your mind, will, and emotions. And your body made up of five senses:

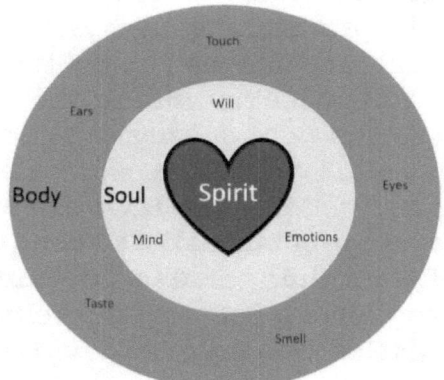

3 parts of a person: Body, Soul, & Spirit

    Anyone out of balance relies far too much on natural sight, with little insight, and almost no foresight - communion with their spirit. Natural sight gains everything from what we see, taste, touch, hear, and smell. Insight adds our mind, will, and emotions into the mix. Foresight is the information we gain from our spirit which is in communion with the Holy Spirit. When Jesus said, "for those with ears to hear..." He was referring to people that have spiritual ears. It is critical that we tap into our creator's heart. God is spirit and we must tune in our spirit to best hear him. There are other ways and God uses them constantly. You hear other people speak His heart; like pastors and teachers, a song on the radio, that perfect social media post at just the right time. He will give you natural signs like rainbows, or birds, or numbers that mean something to you. He is always bombarding you with His heart and His thoughts toward you. God's best is for you to commune with Him in spirit.

God didn't set us here on the earth like orphans. He gave us His Spirit so we can walk with confidence every day. The world, the devil, and people not tuned into His heart may tell you what the temperature is but God is telling you how to change it. Do you live by sight or by faith? If you live by faith you will see what God sees - you will see it with your heart, then you will see it with your eyes. First spirit, then natural, don't get it backwards - you do not see then believe!

This process helps us understand the pain of life's circumstances. We are in a fallen world in the midst of two kingdoms clashing - light and dark. As we advance, showing ourselves as His disciples, He helps us identify the What, Why, and How of needed change. This change sets us free and takes the limits off of God. It keeps us from running around the mulberry bush of worldly expectations in an ever-deepening rut. In the end, this process teaches us to think differently and to see the truth when our natural sight is blind, or to say it in a biblical way; to demolish strongholds.

The Process

What you cannot see, you cannot achieve. God is in the business of giving sight to the blind - that's you and me. Most people live their entire lives only seeing with their natural eyes, weighing what they see with their mind's eyes, and never seeing God's goodness with their spirit's eyes. The next time you run head first into an invisible wall I challenge you to commit yourself to let go of blame and bias. Use the people God has placed in your life to help you digest the evidence around you. Then ask yourself in the presence of the Holy Spirit what do you need to see, what needs line up with Him. **God's greatest desire is not to expose your sin, but to expose His goodness.** He wants to set you free and let you walk according to His purpose in life and life in abundance. He sees the things that bind you and keep you from His best. Listen to Him and live by faith.

Prayer

Father, thank you for loving me. Please help me tap into your heart. Help me see what you see. Help me hear what you're saying. Help me act out of love everywhere I go. Lead me Lord into your good plans. I ask that the world may see your goodness shine through me and my family. I love you Lord.
In Jesus name, Amen.

Nine

Your Purpose

"FOR I know the plans I have for you," declares the LORD, "plans to prosper you and not to harm you, plans to give you hope and a future."
- Jeremiah 29:11

Mark Twain once said, "The two most important days of your life are the day you were born and the day you find out why." The day you find out why you were born is the day you discover your purpose. It is the day the dreams in God's heart concerning you are made known to you. You can do anything, but you cannot do everything. Choose to do what God has for you. He is calling you to play a part in shaping eternity. Each and every one of us has been given a unique design by our Creator, and each have a purpose to fulfill in this life. Our unique

Your Purpose

purposes are the "what" we are called to do. Our unique gifts and talents are "how" we do it. The whole time God is producing the character of His Son in us. As we press in, remember our destiny and purpose is more than a matter of what we do on our journey. It is a matter of who God says we already are, before we do anything or go anywhere. We start our journey best when we start it grounded in our heavenly identity. We are sons and daughters of the living God.

If we do not know our purpose we will flounder in our own abilities and strength, wondering why things are happening, and then spend our energy evading uncomfortable circumstances not knowing what we need or what we should avoid. Think of a child brushing their teeth. If a child is left to decide then he will, like you, weigh the pros and cons. He may think, "I don't like brushing my teeth, I don't like the taste of toothpaste, I'd rather play with toys, I could do this later. What does it matter?" You know it matters but the child can't see what you know. He chooses the path that makes sense to him - the path that is less hassle and pain - not knowing the results of his choice will grow to mature later in life with trips to a dentist fighting tooth decay that hasn't been kept in check. This happens to people every day. Out of sincere love and in answer to their prayers God leads them through situations they need. The catch is they must believe and trust the leading is good or they don't go there. If they don't know it's good or it's God (which is always good) then why go, just like the child thinks, "why brush my teeth?" I know you are in one of two groups:

The first group are those who have discovered God's purpose for their lives and the second are those who haven't. Based on my observation the first group is very small. Most people fall into the second group. It is not enough to just know your purpose, you must also then grow into fulfilling it. The popular path for most is to go with the flow and hope God somehow lets you step in to your purpose like someone steps in a pile of cow dung in a meadow - never saw it coming! That may be a popular belief but it is not biblical. What is biblical is the **path of life**, as stated here;

> "You have made known to me the path of life;
> you will fill me with joy in your presence,
> with eternal pleasures at your right hand."
> - Psalms 16:11

This is also the narrow path. The path that leads to life. The path that unveils your purpose. **Life is a journey and your purpose is unveiled as you walk on the path of life.** It is a process, not a discovery like you found the missing sock from the last laundry load. I want to show you, through His word, how to uncover your God ordained path of life, or your purpose and how to walk in it.

I am sure you understand at this point that the trials and invisible walls we face in life are actually a part of God's process. It is a process designed to mature you spiritually. It is exercise for you on all three levels - spirit, soul, and body. God sees you through His eyes of original intent.

Your Purpose

He sees who you are becoming even though you still need to go through a process of development. God is not impatient with immaturity. In fact, He enjoys relating to you as you grow, just as you do with your children. As you grow and mature, God will test you for the purposes of promoting you to a greater level of influence and to a greater level of maturity. **Your life purpose and destiny depends upon these fundamental daily practices.** Just like the child brushing their teeth. Each trial conquered ends with you being more like Him. An increase in the fruit of the Spirit. An increase in love, joy, peace, patience, goodness, kindness, gentleness, and an increase in self-control. He is preparing you for your destiny. He knows about the lions and bears (1 Samuel 17:34). He knows about the giants after the lions and bears. He is growing you up to walk in victory as you live out your purpose on earth for His glory and your blessing. Much too often people think all they need to do is discover their purpose and go do it. They think it is like they discovered which store in the mall carried their favorite brand of pants, now go buy them. This, at best, is certainly rudimentary and, at worst, just plain wrong.

Whether you know your purpose or not you must enroll in God's higher education program. There is a path He has for you to follow that leads to life abundantly. Don't leave your destiny to chance. Don't try to fulfill your destiny in your own strength, for you are helpless without Him. **This is about your relationship, your walk with God**. This isn't about what you do by yourself or what He does for you by yourself. Don't just sit there praying something changes. Decide right now it is time to change! Declare, "Father, I am at your service. I want to enroll in your education program. Reveal why you have made me - what is my purpose? Prepare me to walk in it - spirit, soul, and body. I choose you, your love, your will over me. I trust you. I praise you. I thank you. May your glory shine through me today and every day. In Jesus name, Amen!" Mark this day in your journal, for today everything changes.

God chose you before he created the world (Ephesians 1:4). This same Almighty creator of the universe thought about you before He made anything. God, who has no limit, thought about you. This is where your purpose began. He thought about your gifts, talents, abilities, and when you would fit right in for His purpose, which is your best! He knows the plans He has for you, but do you know those plans? That is where your purpose lies. As you seek Him, as a disciple you will discover what He has created you for on this earth. The verses following Jeremiah 29:11 say exactly that:

> "Then you will call on me and come and pray to me, and I will listen to you. You will seek me and find me when you seek me with all your heart. I will be found by you," declares the Lord.

You will also be given everything you need -

spirit, soul, and body - to fulfill the passion in your heart as you walk in relationship with Him daily. Do not be deceived thinking that God doesn't really care about the details of your life. He has given you free will, certainly, but He also has a plan for you that is better than anything you may randomly step into. The desire knit into all of our hearts is to fulfill our destiny, God's perfect plan for us. That is where we find the path of life.

Society, in general, treats happiness like air - you can't live without it. Happiness is awesome, but it never should drive your life. It should be a byproduct of your life's choices. Most people put way too high a value on happiness. I love happiness but I don't worship it. Most people will do anything to be happy when honestly the only way to be happy is to be in relationship daily with God. He is your life and He is found only when you are on the path of life. The enemy, the world, and your carnal desires may loudly scream that happiness comes from other things. The truth says narrow is the way to life. I am here to tell you narrow is that same way to happiness. How many years of lying and hollow deceit does someone need to experience before they turn to the truth found in the living God?

It is most critical to remember that we are made up of three parts - body, soul, and spirit. If we only weigh the scale of the natural then we are walking without the whole truth. Just because your body may be happy when you eat cheese cake does not mean your soul or spirit are too. There is much more to your life than

The Purple Pill

what your flesh tells you makes it happy. This is a foundation of the enemy to deceive people. Their own spirit screams that something is wrong and they are not happy, but due to limited understanding we try to resolve unhappiness by quenching our flesh. This is an age old lie the enemy uses - in both directions. Religion is simply acting outwardly with the misplaced hope this will result in an inward change. It is out of order. If the devil can simply get you out of order then he has rendered you ineffective and you are not satisfied, even though you may have Christ in you. You are not satisfied because you are not about the business that is in your heart (spirit) to do. You are trying hard with little or no results. Sound familiar? God is a God of order. There is order in all of creation and this includes you. God is spirit, and those who worship him must worship in spirit and truth. This originates in your spirit, or your heart. Not in any action you may think of for your body to engage in. Trust me, when your heart changes then your actions naturally follow. Power is evident. When actions without the right heart come forth then it is hollow, something is wrong, and there is a lack of His presence and a lack of His power.

The Holy Spirit, I'm sure, has highlighted some routine things in your life to examine in light of His word. He isn't calling for your routine to change, even though it has to. He is calling to your heart with love and truth. Let Him wash you in the water of the word. May your heart respond to His leading in grace and truth. Actions will follow God touching your heart. That is His order. We don't have to hide from him like Adam and Eve. We can let Him place His robe of righteousness on us and circumcise our hearts so we have a heart responsive to Him and not a heart hardened by the deceitfulness of the world. You are in a very good place. This is where you begin to see through the eyes of your heart, not just your natural eyes. You begin to mine the treasure that He has formed in your heart. The passions, desires, and longings that were ordained before the creation of the world.

The Million $ Question

Today, if $1,000,000.00 were deposited into your bank account, what would change?

One morning I woke from a dream where I was in a huge gathering and asked, "If I deposited a million dollars into your account right now, would you do next week what you did last week?" I paused to let the question settle then followed up with, "If your answer is "NO" then be assured you are in need of discovering your "why" in life. Your "why" is found in understanding the creator's original intent for your life." I woke and could see so clearly that if money, a house, car, spouse, or whatever would change your life completely in terms of what you were doing then you are on the wrong path. Those things may help or magnify if we're on the right path, but if you are working every day and have no heart in what you're doing then you need to find out what you were designed to do.

The Purple Pill

For example, if you're currently turning wrenches as a mechanic for a living but after a windfall would never touch a wrench, then you are working for food to survive; motive of fear. You are not working to feed your heart; motive of love. If, after the windfall, you think you may start your own mechanic shop then you would still be doing the same thing. I woke up to the million-dollar question and as I pondered it in my heart I began to see that if we are pursuing our God designed purpose then there isn't anything that would take us away from it. There are things that may help us along the way. What you do is proof of why you do it. If you work for food then when you're full you will have no desire to work. If you work to feed the desires knit in your heart then you will never do anything else and you'll do it with a smile. Today so many people choose to define themselves by things that have no effect whatsoever on who God has created them to be. I call it social noise. We need people to affirm what we do and even why we do it. The problem is when we see someone else doing something different and going a different direction. This causes us to recalculate and question if we're doing the right thing. In reality, this slows you down and keeps you in a land of uncertainty.

There are a myriad of things that influence your purpose. Your parent's occupations and your family shapes an environment that may help grow your purpose like a greenhouse or never water it. People often ask, "what's their purpose" with hopes for the answer, unfortunately the answer is only found from

Your Purpose

seeking the One who designed and knit you together in your mother's womb. I would like to offer some help. When you answer the right questions then what's inside begins to be revealed. The following questions will help lead you to answer the burning question of "what is my purpose?"

The questions you need to answer by asking your Creator are:

What are you good at? This may have nothing to do with your current occupation and that is ok. This question should be fairly easy to answer. If this question is difficult I am sure you are spending way too much time listening to people and seeking their affirmation than you are listening to God's Spirit inside yourself. Remember the fear of man is a snare. Don't worry about what people think. All that really matters is what you think. These are usually things you enjoy doing or would do for others just to "help" even if no one noticed or recognized you work. It may be something that makes things feel "in order."

What do you love to do? Again, this may not line up with what you do day in and day out which is ok. Take the limits off and answer from the heart. The answer here should be fun, easy, and bring a smile to your face. This may be a "desire" in your heart, something you would do if money or education weren't holding you back.

Why do you do what you do? "Why" is a loaded question in a small three-letter package.

Think about what drives you, what inspires you, and what motivates you? Pondering these questions will lead you to answering "why." This will change everything. When you know why then everything else will become clear. Sometimes this is closely related to a "who." Who are you doing it for? You, family, others, or God?

Prayerfully stare at these questions until you have answers. Your answers will reveal your purpose or aim in life. These answers yield three data points to use plotting your course as you sail through life. The struggle of comparing and measuring yourself versus others will shrink to nothing. You will see other "boats" cross your path and won't wonder if you should follow them. You will stay the course and walk in renewed focus, freedom, and joy.

You may spend days on the above paragraph. Fear not, it's worth it. If you are one of those who didn't answer those questions and think you'll just move on then you are making a big mistake. Answering those questions is the most important exercise I could ever imagine you accomplishing. Sincerity with those questions will lead you to serious alignment and peace. You should be really excited right now. I am excited for you. **The revelation I discovered doing what I have presented here for you to do is the "why" will always be rooted in love.** At the end of John 14 Jesus tells the disciples that he is going away and he will send the Holy Spirit to be with them. He goes on to say that the evil one is coming and has no hold

Your Purpose

on him but he comes that the world may learn that Jesus loves the Father and does everything for Him. His "why" is love. Our "why" is also love. When it isn't then we quickly recognize that dry and weary place that so many people live in. When our 'why" is love then streams of living water flow out of our heart and the world sees the glory of God as you walk your path of life and fulfill your purpose.

This is about God pursuing you with love that never quits. He is longing for intimate relationship with you for all eternity. He thought of you before He formed the universe. He knit you together in your mother's womb. He knew you and the depths of your heart. He has brought you here so you can fulfill those longings knit in your heart and fulfill your hearts desires - this is your purpose.

> "The Lord will fulfill his purpose for me
> your love, O Lord, endures forever."
> - Psalms 138:8

Passion results from love. Passion is activated or lit on fire by doing something you love. This points, like a compass, to your purpose. What are the things you would do for free, or that you just love to do? What do you enjoy? Ask the Holy Spirit to reveal the depths of your heart. Take some notes. What do those things have in common? Your purpose is beginning to be revealed with more clarity than ever before. Walking with God is the most exciting thing you can do. It doesn't matter where you are, all that matters is that He is with you. Your purpose can only be revealed by God. Enter His gates with thanksgiving and His courts with praise, then sit down at His feet in communion. Ask Him to reveal your purpose for His glory and LISTEN to His call as you revel in His rest.

This is where His order starts. He begins inside and then goes outward - spirit then soul (mind), then body. It started in a garden to grow into dominion over the whole earth. He starts in your heart, your mind, your body then your whole household, your neighborhood, your city, and your nation. Think of a stone being tossed into a lake causing a ring to emanate out in all directions. That is very much what God is doing with us and our sphere of influence. It grows as we grow in relationship with Him.

Society, and the forces of evil, seems to herd people in the opposite order. The Apostle Peter changed the world, but before he was used to change the world Peter needed to be changed. That is God's order. The push from the world is read it and now go do it or change the world. It is empty and void of power. It does not quench the heart's desire and is void of passion because it is out of order. It may pay the bills but it does nothing past today. As we get in step with God and His order we will be activated and empowered. Your purpose will impact eternity. God created you for eternity and the purpose within you, once fulfilled, will have a lasting effect. **If you aren't doing something that will leave a lasting effect then you are not doing**

God's will, because He is eternal.

You need to master what is uniquely yours. A religious spirit dulls your perception of your uniqueness and causes you to categorize it in a way that makes it useless. Your thumb print, your voice, your calling, your purpose is unique to only you. Wake up. Dwell in the secret place on the inside and watch how the outside aligns and changes to be in agreement with God's plan. You live outside of the boundaries of circumstances that are tormenting those around you. You are carrying the solution to problems that are tormenting them. You have a key within you that only you can unlock what God has for this time to be released on the earth through you, His child.

When you are in your purpose, that thing you were created for, you are not innovating something, or inventing something. You are simply revealing and discovering what was already been scripted by God before He created the foundations of the earth. You are entering into the plan that was already written. When you are living the plan, His purpose, THEN you experience an alignment, a true revival of experiences on all levels - spirit, soul, and body - that mark your life.

This aligning with God's script for your life unveils your purpose and is marked by incredible joy and peace. Honestly, you feel like you are finally living for the first time in your life. You see God has already wrote it, now you are in this place and time in history to reveal His purpose through you!

Prayer

"Father fulfill your heart's desire in my life. Help me trust you every step of the way. Give me ears that hear You. Help me realize it is not just me or just You, but it is living through You and You living through me. Thank you for your love, patience, and redemption. I pray I may fulfill everything you have created me for and the generations after me.

In Jesus name, Amen."

Ten

His Order

STARTS with You

> "As long as the earth endures,
> seedtime and harvest,
> cold and heat,
> summer and winter,
> day and night
> will never cease."
> -Genesis 8:22

God is a Spirit. Everything we see was made from the unseen (Hebrews 11:3). First the spirit then the natural. This is the order of creation, in fact, you could say this is the order of all things.

Genesis chapter one is an illustration of this. The Spirit of God hovered over the waters. God said, "Let there be..., and there was." Each time

His Order

we see from spirit to natural. One thing rarely discussed from these passages is what happened in between hovering over the water and speaking. I believe God first had the thought for light, then spoke. In order for us to mature and fulfill the purpose knit in our heart we must align ourselves with God - get in the right place. We must also heed His order, in His order. God always works from the inside out. He starts in your heart, then your mind or soul, then you see what He put in your heart manifest in our physical world. Ignorance of God's order can leave a person flustered and burnt out. Nothing can be worse than doing the right things in the wrong order, but this is often what we experience and our adversary is quick to lie to us and say God is withholding from us and we must just wait on God. If you are burnt out and frustrated waiting on God there is a problem and it isn't God.

In 1 Timothy chapter 3 Paul is giving instructions for overseers and deacons using the principle discussed above. He exhorts that one must first manage his own family before he can be entrusted with more. This is inside out. First it is your heart, then your family, and moves outward from there. You can jump on a stage first but you'll be out of order and lacking in the power of the Spirit.

The enemy is continually trying to draw our attention to get us out of order. One great example is people doing something to prove their faith. ACTION DOES NOT PRODUCE FAITH. Don't stop taking medicine hoping you will be

The Purple Pill

healed- that's not faith. The opposite is true; faith produces action. When you believe something in your heart then you naturally act accordingly. God's order is critical to walk in life and life in abundance! There is a God ordained order in all of creation. As long as the earth endures, seedtime and harvest, cold and heat, summer and winter, day and night will never cease. The right action at the wrong time or the right action out of sequence leads to barrenness. If you plant seed and then plow you sabotage your own harvest. Seed planted in Winter does not produce a harvest. His order reveals the importance of timing and the sequence of life's events. Understanding your purpose and the process used to guide you will position you in the right place at the right time doing the right thing - Order is restored to your life. A harvest is reaped in due season.

> You can do the right thing at the wrong time and it just doesn't work out.
> You can do the wrong thing at the right time and it just doesn't work out.
> God has a time and place for all things - do you know what and when that is?

That is a really good question. How do you know? You must heed His direction and timing through pressing in to Him and developing an intimate relationship. This is only found in His rest and is void of works. Running around like a dog sniffing for crumbs looking for the things of God does nothing but wear you out. Seek first His Kingdom and righteousness and ALL

His Order

THINGS will be added to you (Matthew 6:33). You seek Him, where you always find rest because His work is finished, and all things are attracted to you. This the exact opposite of the world. They think work harder and get more. In the Kingdom you rest more, not work more.

As you submit to the process He is aligning you to His order for His purpose, which is your best, and brings His Kingdom. A large part of our being anxious or edgy - not at peace - is from being in conflict with God's order. Having all the right directions to a party on note cards is perfect unless you drop the cards and they are out of order. Turning right at the wrong time gets you lost, even if the card said turn right.

"You know what you need?" I can still hear this in my mind. As far back as I can remember people have been saying this to me. My parents, my teachers, my friends, even Dr. Phil. I can't really remember what they said after that though. Strange, isn't it. It seems everyone has an opinion of what you need. Honestly, I am just getting in line. Please keep reading.

> I believe what you want is God's ordained destiny for your life and the life of your family – not to feed sin.

I think about the Israelites with their back against the Red Sea and the Egyptian army bearing down on them. Think about the trial that must have been. Try and put yourself in their shoes. You've just been set free from

The Purple Pill

bondage and left Egypt. It must have been surreal to go from slave to free overnight. There you are. You have your wife and kids and all your possessions. Then you hear the sound of horses and chariots thundering from behind you across the desert. Fear begins to raise its ugly head in your mind. Oh NO!! The Egyptian army is coming to slaughter you. The adrenaline, fear, dismay, must have been almost overwhelming. Your back is against the Red Sea while sure death is coming after you. You know what I want? I want rescued! I want out of there! I want on the other side of the Red Sea! I would give all my belongings for a rowboat. I'm desperate – you get the picture.

You know what I need? I need faith.

In hindsight, it is much easier to see what was needed. In the middle of living life, it's not as easy. Hebrews 11, the great faith chapter, says the Israelites crossed the Red Sea by faith. Therefore, it's easy to see that they needed faith, the Bible says they crossed by faith. It's a piece of cake, thousands of years later with the aid of God's word and a peaceful chair to read it in - Easy.

Unfortunately, it is not that easy when we find ourselves in the midst of life's trials. We long for answers, help, and a way out. **It is at this moment in time when it is so hard to see what you need, will actually help get what you want.** Most people dismiss what they need because they can't see it leads to what they want. God has a divine plan for your life. It is good, perfect, and pleasing. Everyone wants that plan, but then they won't move down the path of what they need. For example, God's plan for David was to be King over Israel. Few people think that David needed to run for his life in the desert for ten to fifteen some odd years. The trials of life produced the character David needed to be able to steward being King. That is why the lion and the bear came before Goliath (the giant). Step by step God is leading us into His perfect plan if we will live by faith and believe Him. Live by faith and trust Him. Live by faith expecting great things.

Another example is Joseph. He had trouble stewarding a dream. He surely wasn't ready to save a nation. Remember when he had a dream that his family would bow down to him. Waking up and telling 11 older brothers they were going to bow down to him was probably not the best way to handle it. It was true, it just was not the right time. God often reveals what's in us, or what we will do. Often someone hears God's plan for their life, like "you will preach the word," then run out and start preaching.

God is all about order and seasons.

There is a right time, a right season for things to come to pass. Jesus came at the right time. He stood up in the synagogue and read from Isaiah 61 at the right time.

Most people hear a word or have a dream/ vision for their lives and then proceed to try

to get what they want rather than trust God is giving them what they need.

That is not living by faith. That young man that heard he will preach the word may just need to work at Walmart and trust God is providing for everything that he needs. Seek God and let Him prepare you to fulfill the calling on your life.

The enemy is all about disorder – chaos. If he can get things out of order then he has frustrated you and short-circuited God's will which is His order. God is Almighty and will hit the God button, like only He can, and give you another opportunity to be aligned. The enemy has just stolen time or postponed your God given destiny. For some this lasts their lifetime. Philippians 1:6 is a wonderful verse, "He who began a good work in you will carry it on to completion, until the day of Christ Jesus." God sees you in light of generations. If Abram's father, Terah, decides to settle in the land of Ur and never make it to Canaan, it's ok. God still loves him. God then says to Abram, "Get up, leave your land and people, and go to the land I will show you." That land is Canaan. Walking with God is the only way to fulfill the cry within your heart - your purpose. We cannot find a shortcut. We must walk with Him, go where He leads, stop when He stops, speak when He says speak. **All of the strange circumstances that seem to pop up and keep you from moving forward are actually the very things you need so you can move forward in victory.** You don't need to avoid them, you need to get over, past, or through them. You need to conquer them. The good news it honestly isn't that hard. It is all about relationship and walking with Him. If we follow His leading we will step right over those hurdles and then smile that we are moving towards our destiny.

Do you live from rest or drama? Once you understand God's order and the importance to be in step with the Spirit then we can begin to enter into a lifestyle, He has prepared for us, that empowers us. Most people live from drama to drama. Doing things according to the world's ways, all the while hoping for God results which quickly leaves one tired and frustrated. It is time to live from rest. Live according to the call being activated within your heart. Psalms 91 describes the person living in God's order. He who dwells in the secret place of the Most High will rest in the shadow of His wings. This is living from rest, this is giving God the throne in your heart. These decisions become easier and more natural the more they're practiced. This impacts the world around you, like a thermostat, instead of letting the world around you live with the status quo. This is is His call to rest in Him. In Him, you will find everything you will ever need and riches unsearchable.

Stewardship

> "Man is buffeted by circumstances so long as he believes himself to be the creature of outside conditions, but when he realizes that he is a creative power, and that he may

command the hidden soil and seeds of his being out of which circumstances grow, he then becomes the rightful master of himself."
- James Allen

    Where the mind goes, the body follows. What you do with what you've been given is stewardship. Walking in purpose, led by grace, resting in His order brings us to a place to truly understand and appreciate stewardship. The world's view and popular teaching on stewardship is to care for another's property like it was your own. The lens of grace reveals that stewardship is taking care of what you've been given, but it is yours and His. Romans 11:36 says, **"For all things are His, through Him, to Him."** This lesson is illustrated in the parable of the prodigal son. Do you remember the son that stayed and didn't blow his inheritance? He was not very happy when his delinquent brother showed up and Dad threw him a party. He was standing outside, livid, when his father went out and pleaded with him. The son said, "Look! All these years I've been slaving for you and never disobeyed your orders. Yet you never gave me even a young goat so I could celebrate with my friends." His father replied, "Son, everything I have is yours." That is awesome! A classic picture of all who do not understand His gospel of grace too. The faithful son did not realize everything was his. Deceived he thought he had to work for it. True stewardship brings us to a place where we believe God, we walk with God, and we use all things for His glory, which is always for our

His Order

blessing.

There is a great story in 2 Kings 4:42 about true stewardship. Elisha is given 20 loaves of bread and he instructs the man to set it before 100 men. His servant asks, "How can I set this before 100 men?" Implying there is nowhere near enough, probably only enough for 20. Elisha answered, "Give it to the people to eat. For this is what the Lord says: 'They will eat and have some left over.'" Then he set it before them, and they ate and had some left over, according to the word of the Lord. **You see when we are given anything from God and use it according to its purpose then He is glorified.** This is exactly when miracles take place. People run all over searching for a formula that results in miracles when God goes to and fro looking for relationship. Miracles glorify God. It is through our relationship He gives us all things. These are for us and the people around us and for God's glory to shine in it. I hope you are seeing the waltz of purpose, order, and stewardship. You cannot dance alone. The beauty of His glory is revealed when you dance with Him.

If miracles glorify God then why aren't their miracles everywhere? Miracles do glorify God and so does stewardship. When we want to be awesome and say, "watch this," then God is sitting this one out. We are taking what is His and using it like the prodigal son used his inheritance - wasting it.

Paul shared the most excellent way to apply the things of God in a productive fruitful way in

The Purple Pill

1 Corinthians 13, the love chapter. Order is awesome but all things must be built upon the foundation of love, for this is the foundation of God. God is love (1 John 4:8). A pitfall to be aware of and a trap most fall into is seeking the things of God, even the ways of God, more than seeking intimate relationship with God who gives us all things. Friends there are way too many brothers and sisters in Christ that live a life lacking in love. "Self" fills the void when there is a lack of love. People begin to be motivated by what "self" is needing, thinking, and desiring versus what love is calling for. People begin to barter with a counterfeit love - they do things expecting to receive things in return. You can never give with a motive to get - that is manipulation and has nothing to do with God. Selfishness quenches the Spirit but few recognize His presence pulling back. Don't just keep going alone thinking you're faithful and in the back of your mind you're hoping God shows up to back your faith filled words even though down deep you know they are spoken with a questionable motive - self before God. That is a bad place to be.

For the things of God are nurtured through relationship not putting your "self" first. God will certainly bless you but it's not intended to stop at you, it must flow through you. Selfishness builds bigger barns to hold to on all that it gets, while godliness expands exponentially. The question comes down to are you doing what is best for you or for God? This is where the rubber meets the road and it's heart check time. To put all things in order then

His Order

God must be first, not self, not even hidden veiled self.

> "Our God is in heaven; he does whatever pleases him.
> But their idols are silver and gold, made by the hands of men.
> They have mouths, but cannot speak, eyes, but they cannot see;
> they have ears, but cannot hear, noses, but they cannot smell;
> they have hands, but cannot feel, feet, but they cannot walk; nor can they utter a sound with their throats.
> Those who make them will be like them, and so will all who trust in them."
> - Psalms 115:3-8

Think about the idol above as self. Those who make them will be like them - yikes! Look at this example from Jesus;

> "During the days of Jesus' life on earth, he offered up prayers and petitions with loud cries and tears to the one who could save him from death, and he was heard because of his reverent submission."
> - Hebrews 5:7

What if people aren't in reverent submission? What if they have self not submitted to God? Would it be safe to say due to the lack of reverent submission they are not heard? That's sobering and certainly explains a lot about the periods of silence. The dictionary defines Bias as a

The Purple Pill

particular tendency, trend, inclination, feeling, or opinion, especially one that is preconceived or unreasoned.

Anytime a person puts their interests in front of God they are then looking through lens of bias which wrongly influences their choices. Bias blinds. There is a twisting of the truth or an incomplete view of it. You see it all the time when people buy or sell something. A seller doesn't notice the dents on a car just what the book value of a perfect car is, and it goes on and on.

The roots of bias are found in one's desires and past experiences. Bias, simply, is self-serving. e.g. people from Denver have a bias for Denver sports teams. Bias builds walls built in our thinking to protect us. There is a difference between bias, not being true, and unbiased where truth speaks for itself. What we think is protecting us is actually a dreadfully serious problem here. Bias weakens you spiritually and keeps you from the good things of God.

Bias leads people to make decisions that are self-serving which quenches the Spirit and leads to dryness of life. I believe a great measure of bias is Joy. No joy means loads of bias. Complete joy means no bias. Serving the Lord brings joy, serving yourself skews true joy to happiness which is self-serving. In the end, it brings misery. The joy of the Lord is your strength - not the joy of you. Bias is actually the enemy of the truth which will set you free. The evidence of God in a life is the fruit of the Spirit - love, peace, and joy (Galatians 5:22).

Love is kind, love honors, love keeps no record of wrongs, **love is not self-seeking**, love always protects, love always trusts, love always hopes, love always perseveres, and LOVE NEVER FAILS. When your motive is love then the world around you is getting a glimpse God (not you). This brings Him glory. Love puts self after God, after your spouse and family, after your neighbor. God loves you so you don't need to fear from lack. The catch here is often the way people process, they hear, "self last, live by love." Many, because of the influence of darkness and the ways of the world, take this to mean they are worth less than what they put before them, i.e. others. This is a lie and a terrible stronghold the enemy tries to fortify in order to steal all the good things God has for you when living a life of love shining His glory. Scripture tells us we must love our neighbor as our self. If we put some strange value hierarchy to the way we love then we have a huge problem because we aren't loving our self. We have to understand how loved we are first in order to love anyone else! Those struggling to know in their depths that God loves them and they lack no good thing will seek after position, gifts, and the things of God to show themselves awesome. God is not on that bus. That bus has "religion" on the front of it and is racing out of control to a pit of fire. The Apostle Paul, in 1 Corinthians 13 reminds us if a man is awesome - if he can woo people with prophecy, fathom all mysteries, if he has faith that moves mountains but is void of love, then he is NOTHING. If he gives all that he has, yet is not motivated by love - he gains NOTHING.

Walking in God's order and stewarding all He has graciously blessed us with must always be motivated and built on a foundation of love. If anyone lives a life lacking in love, then it is a life lacking in God. Living as a child of God is really pretty easy. You don't have to have a book full of do's and don'ts, you don't have to remember some complex order of things to live a life full of love. Love well and God will live through you well and you will thrive in life.

Prayer
"Lord God, I pray for your Spirit to settle in my heart your purpose, your order and stewardship. May I rest in your love, may I know and trust you for you are love. I believe you are not going to give me anything that will hurt or destroy me. Trials I face are for my good and are building me up and growing me closer to you. I know you are a God of order and I am a part of that order. Father I ask you to remove anything that may be hindering me to dance with you fulfilling my purpose, for your glory. Thank you for living through me and setting me free. Use me to impart your good, pleasing and perfect will everywhere I go.
In Jesus name, Amen!"

Eleven

His Kingdom

THE Kingdom and your reward both come by having the audacity to believe God.

Our loving Father gently raises a mirror so we can see a clear reflection of ourselves in light of His truth. We see what we see and we see what He sees. He always sees what's in His heart for that is what you will be. In the midst of this the enemy, void of power unless we yield it to him, comes bending and twisting the mirror altering the reflection to kill, steal, and destroy. As we fit the armor of God on and begin to wield the sword of the Spirit we find it awkward and clunky at first, but with the Spirit's help it begins to feel natural as we join Him in a beautiful waltz, we ebb and flow with the rhythms of His grace. Glancing toward our past we see one victory after another as we heed the call God has put on our life. Test after test purifies our hearts. Our reflection is beginning to look a whole lot like Jesus. Discovering our purpose, since the creation of the world, we walk with a true heart of stewardship for all things are ours and all things are His. In His time, in His order, as we walk we are born into Godly promotion.

Promotion is the result of transition - moving from one level to the next. To successfully press through transition to find promotion is only correctly done through our partnership with God. We each play a part. There is a counterfeit out there that people can find and press through by education, bribes, earthly wisdom, or flattery but that promotion always results in lifelessness. It is dry and lonely. There is no satisfaction in it other than temporal fleshly satisfaction that dries up in days not years. Nothing that stands the test of time. Partnering with God on our sojourn we find our job is to be faithful and live a life of love. Love God and love your neighbor like yourself. This is a place of rest. This is not a formula or list of endless tasks that drain the life out of you. This is life with God, full of joy, peace, and all of the wonderful fruit of the Spirit. Resting in what He has done and availed to us by His grace.

God's job is to prepare us for His promotion. His love for us never ends and He would never promote us if it would hurt us. The world will throw someone on stage or in a place of authority before they are ready, not knowing or caring that it is causing more pain than blessing. You wouldn't give your child a position of top chef when you knew they couldn't use a knife without cutting themselves, much less cook. Do you think God would? He may put the desire inside but then He ensures you are prepared for it when promotion comes.

Far too often people mistake the need for information or knowledge as the way to promotion. Knowledge is awesome and needed but it is not a prerequisite for promotion. God is all about using the weak and foolish all of the time. I'm encouraged every time I think about how good God is. He uses the weak and foolish to shame the strong and wise - guess what? I'm qualified and so are you! You may wonder what, then, are the pre-requisites to promotion? Three things: Faith, Hope, and Love.

> "And without faith it is impossible to please God, because anyone who comes to him must believe that he exists and that he rewards those who earnestly seek him."
> - Hebrews 11:6

Faith is the fuel for your life. We live by faith. We walk by faith. We see by faith. We are saved by grace through faith. We must come to the place where we believe what God says over what we think, sense, or see. Everything in the natural, physical world changes. It is a fact people cannot walk on water yet Jesus did and so did Peter.

Never let facts confuse the Truth. Believing facts are truth closes the door on faith.

"Without weakening in his faith, he faced the fact that his body was as good as dead—since he was about a hundred years old—and that Sarah's womb was also dead. Yet he did not waver through unbelief regarding the promise of God, but was strengthened in his faith and gave glory to God."
- Romans 4:19-20

His words, which are spirit, never change. Everything we see was made from the unseen, from His spoken word. Take a moment and read Genesis 1 - "And God said...." Now read Hebrews 11 (out-loud), the faith chapter. Verse one tells us Faith is being sure of what we hope for and certain of what we do not see. Hope is confident expectation. We must have a joyful expectation (hope) that what God said is coming to pass even if the world won't confirm it; even if we can't see it. Faith cannot exist without hope. Everything God has for us is already available in the spiritual realm and we access it by faith.

"His divine power has given us everything we need for life and godliness through our knowledge of him who called us by his own glory and goodness."
- 2 Peter 1:3

Love: The Key to the Kingdom

Love God and love your neighbor like yourself.

Love is the key to the Kingdom. Faith works

The Purple Pill

by love (Galatians 4:6). Before divine promotion we find love - love for God, and love for yourself - this empowers you to love others. What you are aware of, or have, you can impart. The world promotes people who can severely lack love - God does not. The basic building block of your design was for relationship, first with God, then others. This where love leads the way. Very often people think knowledge is power because they then use it to manipulate others to get something they want. That is not love and that is not the purpose of knowledge. Here is the bottom line. We all follow a leader and have the need to follow and lead in one capacity or another. Your life cannot be complete sitting in a closet alone even with an iPad :) Your destiny involves being in alignment with the right people, at the right time.

There are only two ways to lead; manipulate or inspire.

Manipulation imposes the leader's will upon people to influence them to choose an action that benefits the leader. Tactics could be fear, fact, lies, deceit - it is all with an underlying guise to control outcome for their good, their purpose.

Inspiration connects people's hearts. The leader shares their heart and people are inspired by what's in them that connects with the leader. Their dormant beliefs deep in their heart come alive. **People then choose to act for their benefit,** not the leaders, to align themselves and follow. Good leaders know people are attracted not pursued. Your "why" connects and aligns with the desires of their heart. This results in a beautiful alignment that only God could orchestrate - free from control.

God calls us, often completely unqualified for the call, then begins to share what's in His heart for our life. His love draws us to seek Him, we then receive images, ideas, hopes, and dreams. These are His desires and your future based on His love. He is painting a picture of a reality you are going to possess. He qualifies the unqualified. The living God always works from the inside out. He starts with your heart, then your family, then your sphere of influence. Changing the world around you will also manifest opposition to the things of God. You don't bind the strong man opposing you when you show up. You bind the strong man before you get there. The stronger man is the one who binds. It is strength, in Christ, not the act of binding that enables you to plunder his house and manifest God's will in your home, neighborhood, city, and on earth.

Favor opens doors that you walk through by faith. What I mean by this is seeing what God is doing and doing it, just like Jesus did. You will then find yourself in a position to make an impact in your environment. Speaking with wisdom, motivated by love, and being led by the Spirit will enable you to seize the moment and embrace God's promotion.

You carry an authority in you, within your Godly assignment, that will magnetically cause alignments to happen. You will access God's gifts and resources within your assignment, providing you show up in the humility and the love of God. In Ephesians (3:18) the Apostle Paul is praying that "you may have power, together with all the saints, to grasp how wide and long and high and deep is the love of Christ." Did you notice it takes power to grasp God's love. This is not just in your mind - Love is spirit and unleashes God's power. This is a process that never ends. People may doubt this because of the lack of promotion they see and the depth of the rut they are living in. This process works and never ends, but if you do not play your part - live a life of love - then the process stalls and you are repeatedly presented with one opportunity to love after another. Bypassing those opportunities to love results in a hardness of heart and desperate need to repent. We do not want people to say about us what Jesus described as the love of most will grow cold.

In the parable of the sower, Matthew 13, Jesus describes a man casting seed out on the ground. Some fell on rocky ground and the birds ate it. Some fell on shallow ground and immediately started to grow but the heat of the sun scorched it. Some fell on soil but was choked by weeds so it could not grow. And other seed fell on good ground that grew and produced a crop 30, 60, or 100 times what was sown. The disciples ask Jesus to explain it, so He does. Here is my synopsis;

The sower sows the word. I remind you that Jesus is the living word (John 1), and God is love (1 John 4:8).

Sowing the word therefore is sowing love.

To produce a crop, it must find good soil - your heart must be a heart where love may flourish. A heart that believes God. A heart that is guarded from the worries of life and deceitfulness of wealth. Here is where you find His promotion - what's sown is multiplied 30, 60, and 100 times.

> "This is the confidence we have in approaching God: that if we ask anything according to his will, he hears us. And if we know that he hears us—whatever we ask—we know that we have what we asked of him."
> 1 John 5:14c-15

According to His will is according to LOVE. Anything less he doesn't even hear. Living a life of love will lead you to, as God intended, your calling and promotion in life and His abundance. People will see you and the light of God shining from you. Yield to God's loving gentleness and watch the revival that follows you everywhere you go! **The result of His promotion for you is His Kingdom on the earth!**

His Kingdom Come

> "The seventh angel sounded his trumpet, and there were loud voices in heaven, which said: "The kingdom of the world has become the kingdom of our Lord and of his Christ, and he will reign for ever and ever."'

- Revelation 11:15

John G. Lake said:
"... the objective of Christianity is the kingdom of the Lord and Savior Jesus Christ in this world."

The church is Christ's ecclesia—His government on the earth. The gospel of the Kingdom is the practical dominion of Christ manifest through His anointed ones living out their God ordained purpose on the earth by loving like Jesus did. This is the Kingdom that cannot be shaken. The kingdom of darkness is getting shaken because God's saints, the kings of the earth, motivated by love, are speaking His heart, and His will, everywhere they go. When light shines, darkness flees or you could say is shaken and flees.

You want a theology that empowers you as the world is shaken and trouble increases. You are not here to escape to heaven. Jesus had authority in heaven, authority on earth, and authority in hell. His kingdom in heaven was brought to earth. He came as a man to set us free to walk in our God given authority free from sin and darkness. You are here to bring His Kingdom of love to the earth. You are here to prepare Jesus' inheritance of people and nations on earth. Heaven on earth. The gospel of the Kingdom releases you to be at the epicenter of all culture that we might shine with God's love and bring heaven to earth. **The church is not a building but the ecclesia, the called-out ones,**

His Kingdom

to govern with a heart of love and bring order to earth. We are the priests, prophets and kings who are called as a company, a called-out company, to cover the Earth with God's glory in Christ, and to fill the Earth with that glory. Because we are the body of Christ. Go and make disciples. Go and have dominion over all the earth. Fulfill your Fathers desire and let life and life in abundance drip off of you everywhere your foot treads. Fulfill what burns within your heart. Glorify God. We focus on the Kingdom and He builds the church. Taste heaven at church and unpack the kingdom everywhere you live, work, and play. Heaven is invading earth. Jesus Christ is coming and the antichrist is manifesting. Satan's power is being displaced. The shaking is from God. The glory of God shall be seen on you. In gross darkness is when light shines brightest. Walking in God's promotion will attract followers. People will be attracted to the fruit in your life, the Jesus in you. You will help them discover the purpose knit in their heart and align themselves to walk in His blessing and bring His glory to the earth.

> "Arise, shine, for your light has come,
> and the glory of the LORD rises upon you.
> See, darkness covers the earth
> and thick darkness is over the peoples,
> but the LORD rises upon you
> and his glory appears over you.
> Nations will come to your light,
> and kings to the brightness of your dawn.
> - Isaiah 60:1-3

The Purple Pill

I look forward to hearing many great success stories from you that glorify Jesus. May God bless you, guide you, fill you with wisdom, fulfill the desires of your heart, and protect you and your whole family as you walk with Him into more than you could ever hope, think, or imagine! In Jesus name, Amen.

I leave you with one last quote;

> "Rule with the heart of a servant, and serve with the heart of king."
> -Pastor Bill Johnson

Author Page

Rob has a reputation for prophetic insight and revelation that brings living water to dry ground. Along the lines of Gideon, he believes many others are more qualified to share God's heart, but once again God chooses the weak and foolish things to bring His heart's desire to earth.

Rob and his wife Lesa

Author

The best way to contact Rob is by email rob@robstatham.com or twitter @RobertEStatham.

Thank you for reading The Purple Pill. We love feedback. Please leave a review on Amazon when it's convenient.

May God bless and prosper you abundantly so the whole world may see God's glory.

The Purple Pill
God's call for His bride to make herself ready.

Copyright © 2017 Robert E. Statham

The Purple Pill

www.ingramcontent.com/pod-product-compliance
Lightning Source LLC
Chambersburg PA
CBHW020615300426
44113CB00007B/658